Victoria

500 CHRISTMAS IDEAS

Celebrate the Season in Splendor

Victoria

500 & CHRISTMAS IDEAS

Celebrate the Season in Splendor

KIMBERLY MEISNER

HEARST BOOKS
A division of Sterling Publishing Co., Inc.

New York / London
www.sterlingpublishing.com

Design by Celia Fuller
Floral background ©iStockphoto.com/Yuliya Marozava

Library of Congress Cataloging-in-Publication Data
Meisner, Kimberly.
Victoria, 500 Christmas ideas : celebrate the season in splendor / Kimberly Meisner.
  p. cm.
Includes bibliographical references and index.
ISBN 978-1-58816-766-8 (hardcover : alk. paper) 1. Christmas decorations. 2. Handicraft. 3. Christmas cookery. I. Victoria (New York, N.Y.) II. Title.
TT900.C4M393 2009
745.594'12—dc22

                                                                        2008050295

10 9 8 7 6 5 4 3 2 1

Published by Hearst Books
A Division of Sterling Publishing Co., Inc.
387 Park Avenue South, New York, NY 10016

Victoria and Hearst Books are trademarks of Hearst Communications, Inc.

www.victoriamag.com

For information about custom editions, special sales, premium and corporate purchases, please contact Sterling Special Sales Department at 800-805-5489 or specialsales@sterlingpublishing.com.

Distributed in Canada by Sterling Publishing
c/o Canadian Manda Group, 165 Dufferin Street
Toronto, Ontario, Canada M6K 3H6

Distributed in Australia by Capricorn Link (Australia) Pty. Ltd.
P.O. Box 704, Windsor, NSW 2756 Australia

Manufactured in China

Sterling ISBN 978-1-58816-766-8
Book Club Edition ISBN 978-1-58816-810-8

CONTENTS

INTRODUCTION

THE CHRISTMAS SEASON IS FILLED WITH CELEBRATIONS and traditions that bring us together: caroling, gift giving, cooking with friends and family, and, of course, the tree and all its trimmings. Family traditions play a vital role at Christmastime. Our loved ones treasure the season's rituals: the familiar wreath on the door, the heirloom angel on the tree, and the favorite cast of cookies and characters, year after year. These time-honored traditions are an indispensable piece of our celebrations and our decorations. And yet within this familiar framework, endless new possibilities await.

Every November, we unpack boxes of ornaments we greet like dear friends, and hold in our hands decorations that have served as the backdrop to many of our most cherished memories. Every family's Christmas decorations are as precious and personal as the family members themselves. As essential as these treasures are, however, they have the potential to grow a bit stagnant over time. Year after year, they make us feel excited, cozy, nostalgic…and occasionally, a bit bogged down. However, there is always a fresh, new way to interpret any Christmas tradition. And that is what this book is all about.

Our Christmas decorations are always personal to us: to our families, our homes, our tastes. But this Christmas, let them reflect something more: your life, your mood, your dreams, your latest whim. Explore the photographs and ideas in this book, and then liberate yourself to do something new. What means the most to you? What have you been secretly longing to try? Maybe you'd like to pare down, keep things simple and elegant, and decorate with a few, well-chosen pieces illuminated only by candlelight. Or maybe you want to decorate with more intention, more color, more flowers, more everything. Perhaps you'd like to bring a sense of history to your tree, with some home-made or vintage ornaments and cherished family photos tucked in the branches—or maybe this year it's time for something completely fresh and new, like a tree done all in silver and white, or dressed in shimmering clusters of handblown glass. Maybe you are searching for new ways to make your guests feel warm and welcome in your home, or for a chic new approach to your host gifts.

Whatever your heart's desire is this Christmas, enjoy meandering through these pages, full of options and ideas—from simple notions to enjoyable craft projects, from tiny details to bold strokes, and from the cleanest designs to the most ornate. Seek out images that speak to you and ideas that inspire. Look to this past year and what it has brought for you and your family. Did you move to a new home? Have a baby? Make a life change? Did you organize some old family photos? Plant a new garden? There is inspiration to be found in surprising places for your holiday decor.

Really express yourself in your trimmings this year, even while you decorate with tried and true favorites. Beloved ornaments can be moved from their traditional spots on the tree and gathered in a glass apothecary jar or silver compote for a lovely new place of honor. Ordinary green wreaths can be graced with handfuls of herbs and flowers from the garden or nursery, transforming them into a lush display. Familiar table settings become a winter wonderland when strewn with white roses, champagne–pink candles, delicate silver bows, and gleaming porcelain fruits on a snowy–white chenille cloth.

Whether you deck your tree in silver and gold or in pinecones and popcorn; whether you top your table with an artful arrangement of crystal and roses or a cozy tumble of herbs and apples; whether you wrap your gifts with ornate organdy bows or simple knots of twine — allow the photos and tips in these pages to open up a new world of possibility for you, to design the Christmas of your dreams.

HOME FOR CHRISTMAS

Entrances
and Hallways

1

*

Bedeck a wooden doorway
with a festive Scottish flair,
hanging plaid and woolen
stockings smartly dressed with
cuffs and buttons to fill
with gifts and sprigs of heather,
holly, and berries.

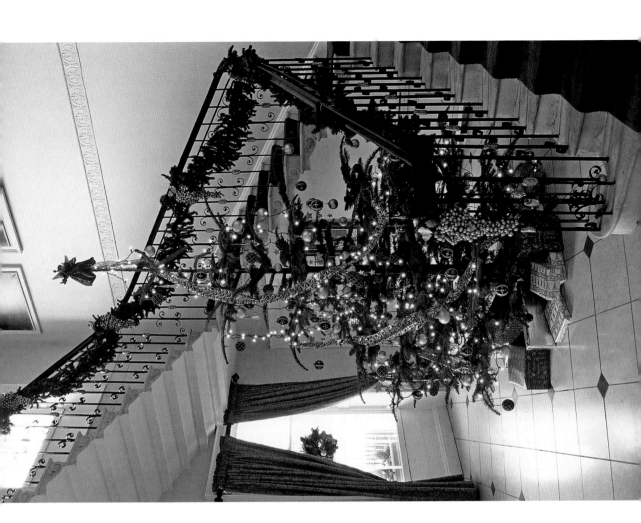

2

Festoon a sweeping staircase with fragrant swags of balsam accented by bounteous bunches of golden berries.

3

Stir anticipation for the gala to come by adorning your foyer with its own tree, decked in golden finery and filled with the promise of the evening.

4

Even an entrance in colonial yellows and blues becomes a cheery Christmas threshold when surrounded by garlands of greens dotted with pinecones and red ribbon.

5

Cluster creamy candles of rolled beeswax, which have a natural scent, are dripless, and burn longer than paraffin candles. ▼

6

Embrace the celestial decorating opportunities of a grand staircase. This toasted orange stair hall is a forest of firs, littered with enticing ivory bags full of mysterious gifts.

7

Use light to create atmosphere in unexpected places. Here, the uncarpeted staircase becomes an enchanted passageway when lined with delicate glass votives.

8

*

Bring a delicate sparkle to your table or hall with an unexpected piece, like this abstract tree with pale green bits of glass and a light dusting of gold glitter.

When festooning a white painted banister, try a lively natural color scheme of greens, blues, ivory, and a touch of plum. Cedar forms the base of this garland, providing a dark, feathery backdrop for contrasting seed-pods, greenery, and luscious blooms of white amaryllis at the top of the newel post.

10

*

Warm the hearts of visitors with a happy message to greet them as they enter your home and a glowing red star to light their way.

11

✴

When your home decor flows well with your holiday decorations, a little can go a long way. These powerful red pillows so beautifully complement the red holly berries in the wreath that nothing more is needed to ready this stately entrance hall for Christmas. ▼

12

✴

Bestow the mirror in your entrance hall a fluid crown of greens. The exquisite etchings on this beveled glass mirror sparkle like icy boughs on a winter day.

13
✳

Deck your entrance with an earth-toned garland fashioned of nuts, ponderosa pinecones, and miniature gourds.

14
✳

Give your staircase special treatment by tucking aromatic dried fruits, spices, and pinecones into a lush garland and securing it along the banister with golden rope.

15
✳

Turn holiday bows into colorful bouquets by mixing ribbons of different textures and hues. Here, shimmering loops of champagne-colored organdy soften a red velvet ribbon trimmed with gold wire.

Living Spaces

* 16

Use a box brimming with colorful wrapping paper, ribbons, and rickrack as a decorative touch, keeping cherished wrappings in the spotlight long after they've been ripped off the gifts.

17

✳

In a smaller house, or one that includes children or pets, consider elevating Christmas with a tabletop tree — like this live blue spruce with its root-ball wrapped with twine and toile. A home-painted cupboard works as a tree stand.

18

✳

Save the ornaments and lights for other areas of your home. Classic and easy homemade trimmings like these paper snowflakes, pinecones, and pipe cleaner garland give a tree individuality and charm, as do unexpected additions like the feathers and glittering chandelier crystals.

Bigger is not necessarily better: when choosing a tree, keep in mind the space where it will spend the holiday. This tree has a wonderfully full base for decorating, while its thin top allows for a clear view of the lovely details and decorations on the mantel and walls beyond.

19
✳

20
✳

Embrace a theme that brings you joy and spread it throughout your decorations. Here, the cheerful comfort of apples moves from candles on the mantel to ornaments in the tree to a large wooden bowl of juicy delights by the hearth.

21

✳

Enhance the beauty of your Christmas decorations by supplementing them with other items in your home. Here, a series of gathered candlesticks beautifully reflects the pine greens and the subtle jewel tones of the fruits in the wreath and garland.

22

Create a place of respite for members of your household who may not be as enamored of flowers, candles, and glittering lights. With the help of mellow-toned accessories, comfy pillows, and a tufted chair, any corner can become a masculine retreat.

23

Celebrate the literary treasures of the Christmas season by propping open a favorite picture book for all to enjoy. This lovely chair, upholstered in the same reds and creams as the pillow and wallpaper, provides a welcoming corner to escape into heartwarming stories of Christmas. ▼

24
*

Amid lush gatherings of fragrant spruce and delicate white flowers, a fluffy sheep and her faithful ram keep watch.

25
*

It would be natural to hesitate to hang a stocking as dressy as this treasure stitched with bead-embroidered fabric. Instead, lay it delicately on the living room sofa. However, no stocking is too fancy to be filled with gifts. ▼

26

✳

Festoon a spot near your tree with swags of greenery and flowers to complement the tree's decorations and to carry its convivial air throughout the room.

27

✳

Create festive and comfortable nooks near the tree with enough seating for family members and guests who may choose not to sit on the floor for the opening of gifts on Christmas morning.

28

✳

Drape a small curtain of greens on the side of a chair with a simple, unfussy ribbon for a lovely, natural touch. ▶

29
✳

Vivid satin hearts set out on an ivory creamware plate catch the eye with their nontraditional design, yet perfectly capture the romantic, old-world feeling of Christmas. ▼

30
✳

To maintain a light, airy feel in your home, opt for trays lined with fresh fruit, a glass vase of calla lilies, and a few shiny, pale-colored ornaments loosely tied with sheer ribbon.

Dining Rooms and Kitchens

✳

31

Vintage cranberry glass, in all its elegance, is hard to find but worth the effort. This belle epoque etched- and cut-crystal decanter is made by hand, using a centuries-old layering method — twenty-two people were involved in producing each piece. If you are lucky enough to uncover one, give it its due on a rich red patent leather place mat with leather holly-sprig napkin rings.

32

✳

If you are doing some baking this Christmas, don't rush your creations into Tupperware. Let the abundance of your cookies, biscuits, and fresh country bread fill your kitchen with the delectable aromas and textures of the holidays.

33

Give your kitchen a homey Christmas background by displaying your vintage canisters—or tins like these that have been deliberately chipped and dented to perfectly replicate the originals—on counters covered by a simple green-checked fabric.

34

Every surface in the house has the potential to fit subtly into the decorations of the home. A few well-placed glass votives and fresh sprigs of pine on this zinc-topped table turn the preparations for dessert into a lovely holiday display.

35

Drape your kitchen windows
with garlands of dried apple slices
and bunches of cinnamon sticks
tied with raffia, and string them
under a bower of greens for a
lovely combination of fragrances.

36

Fill chubby glass masonry jars
with sprigs of your favorite herbs
and keep them in the kitchen for
easy access while cooking, as well
as for a lively jolt of fragrance
and color.

37

Stow away your everyday china
and crystal until January comes,
so beautiful Christmas china and
collections — like these wonderful
nutcrackers — can be given their
due and properly displayed
throughout your hutches and
cabinets.

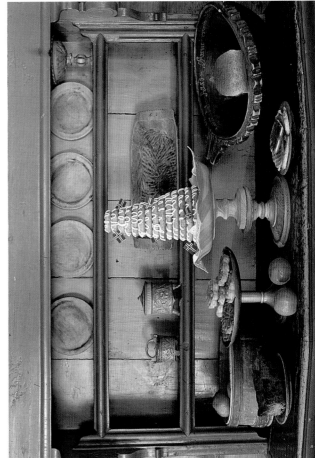

38
✳

Turn a year-round display into a Christmas tableau by hanging an ornament and a sprig of greens on a festive ribbon from the top of a hutch or shelves.

39
✳

Fill an antique sideboard with your family's traditional sweets of the season; in this Norwegian home, that includes tarts, cookies, and a towering garland cake.

40

An abundance of luscious pine needs nothing but a few red accents — ornaments, ribbons, candles, flowers — to highlight its natural beauty. Here, a snowy backdrop of white on white enlivens the idyllic chorus of reds and greens.

41

Brighten up your table with a surprising choice of flowers, like these bright red cyclamens and gerbera daisies.

42

Suspend a bounty of wreaths in front of a large window using long loops of thick, strong ribbon.

43
*

Warm up any table with an angel-topped chandelier — filled with candles, lined with rich boxwood, and draped with checked ribbon. A wire basket filled with fresh apples is all the centerpiece you'll need.

All Through
the House

✴ 44

Discover the hidden beauty
that hides in the corners of your
home. These gleaming copper
watering cans, when displayed
with mercury glass apple and
pear ornaments with copper
fittings and leaves, give off a
lovely holiday glow.

✴ 45

Spread Christmas cheer to every
room in the house. In this home
office, amaryllis adds a quick and
easy holiday touch. ▼

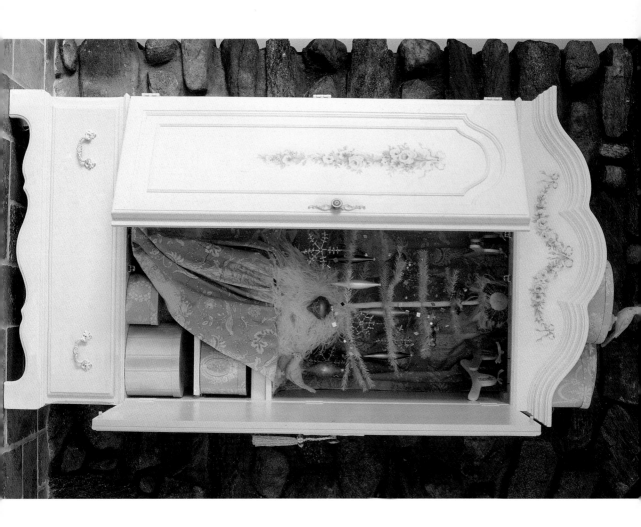

46

Remember the hidden spaces in your home, as they can offer the ideal space to try something new. Inside of this painted armoire, a delicate white feather tree gleams with blue ornaments and softly complements the hues of the draped fabric and hat boxes.

47

Line a white wooden shelf with a forest of straw-colored bottle-brush trees from the 1930s. ▼

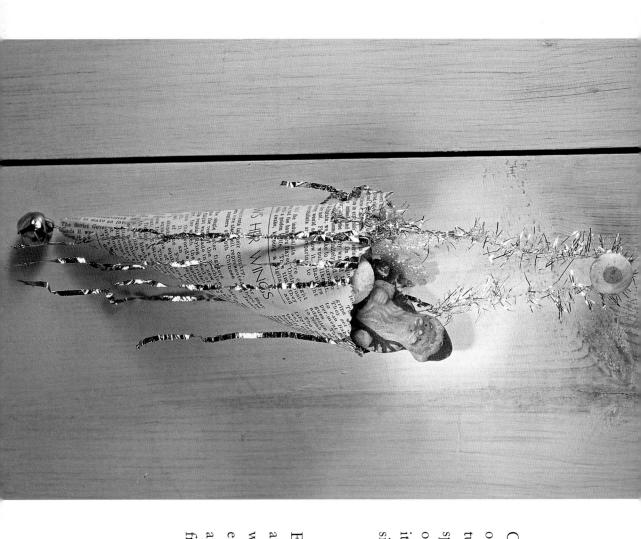

48

Give a plain cabinet door a bit of vintage Christmas cheer by tucking a little Santa and some sparkly tinsel into a cozy cone of old newsprint and hanging it on the knob with a thin silver garland.

49

Embrace a simple setting and line your windowsills with boughs of White Pine embellished with polished apples and berries. Their sweet fragrance will fill the room. ▼

50

✳

A pyramid of forced paperwhites in tiered bowls nestles in greenery against frosty window panes where blossoms linger longest without fading. ▼

51

✳

Drape deep-green boughs to give this silver chandelier an air of elegance and grandeur.

52
✳

Add a loving touch to frosted windowpanes. Tuck heart-shaped cookies into glassine envelopes, numbered for the days of Advent with glued-on daisies, mother-of-pearl buttons, and button-head mums. Hang with ribbons and vintage gold bullion stars. ▼

53
✳

Embrace the use of hearts in your holiday trimmings. This symbol of love, hope, and joy is as welcome at Christmas as it is on Valentine's Day. ▶

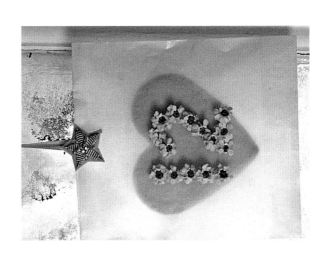

54
✳

Light a flight of unused stairs or an out-of-the-way series of shelves with a merry procession of votive candles and extra clippings from the tree. ▶

55
*

A trio of friendly snowmen bring cheer to any room. These were handmade with durable beeswax — set in chocolate molds and then painted. ▼

56
*

Say Noel with a bounty of ornamental balls. Fill a basket to bursting with translucent and glitter-striped balls handblown and handmade by artisans.

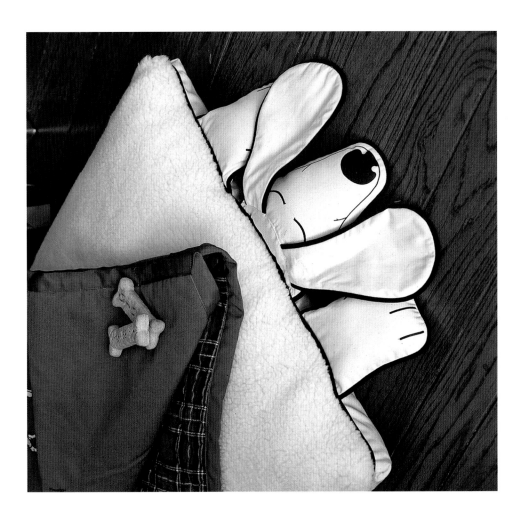

57
✳

A chorus of handblown glass ornaments sings a joyful song of color and light when dangled artfully in front of a sunny window with sheer lace curtains. ▼

58
✳

Pamper your pets at Christmas: lay out cozy quilts with red tartan linings and snuggly fleece beds.

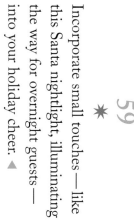

59

Incorporate small touches — like this Santa nightlight, illuminating the way for overnight guests — into your holiday cheer. ▲

60

Blanket your home in the textures of nature. Here, pinecones, twine, bark, and burlap surround fragrant boughs of pine for the cozy atmosphere of an authentic woodland Christmas. ▼

61

※

Hide presents in potpourri-filled baskets crowned with cones, ivy, apples, and greenery to create two gifts in one.

62

※

Include fragrant arborvitae—an evergreen from the cypress family—in your holiday decorations. Unlike its prickly cousins, it is soft to the touch, allowing for easy manipulation.

Nothing is more elegant than the graceful wooden curves of well-tended musical instruments. If you have them in your home, consider placing your violin, harp, or grand piano at center stage in this year's decorations.

63

✳

64

✳

To capture the glorious winter light from the warmth of your home, save your most luminescent ornaments for window dressing. Suspend them in front of sunny windows with shimmering organza ribbon.

65

✳

Create an herb lover's garland fashioned of thyme and rosemary, along with sprigs of fresh bay leaves. Contrast their deep green with lacy gray artemesia, as well as the flowers of lavender, calamint, marjoram, and the pale beauty of white roses.

For collectors of Santa figurines and other icons of Christmas, every table, mantel, and corner of the tree can hold irresistible scenes of wonderment and delight.

✳
66

✳
67

A sturdy brown wicker trunk is a wonderful place for a warm tableau of pastoral hues. Here, salmon-colored roses and an ivy Christmas tree, both nestled snugly in terra-cotta pots, flank a tray of pinecones. A framed botanical print in the center completes the bucolic display. ▼

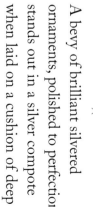

68

A bevy of brilliant silvered ornaments, polished to perfection, stands out in a silver compote when laid on a cushion of deep green boxwood.

69
✳

Transform an open window into a bright tableau of holiday joy. Here, surrounded by earthly glories, an angel's trumpet heralds the gifts of Christmas.

70
✳

For a lush accent or backdrop to floral arrangements, use moss to coat a large Styrofoam ball covered in burlap. Floral pins will keep the moss sheets in place, and misting will keep them green.

71

Bright amaryllis and paperwhites, freshly cut and brimming from simple glass containers, look beautiful with no arrangement or adornment.

72

Find inspiration for your holiday decorations in the themes already present in your home. Here, simply chic white serving dishes surrounded by glass containers and candlesticks perfectly illuminate the white picture frames and crystal chandelier.

Spice up your coatrack with a jaunty seasonal accent. A felt snowman on skis next to a glittering snowflake will add a spark of winter fun to your mudroom.

74

✳

Give a bronze candelabra an air of mystique by adorning it with sparkling chandelier crystals and twilight blue ribbons.

75

✳

The pure light of day is sometimes the best way to exhibit the complex beauty of handblown glass ornaments. ▼

76

For a delicately detailed display,
root a diminutive 1930s bottle-
brush tree in a pink lusterware
cup with a sprinkling of small
pinecones. Set it atop a pairing
of creamware plates, where a
dusting of artificial snow will
glow in their buttery warmth.

77

✳

Use your creativity and include any household treasure you'd like in your trimmings. A tiny necklace of greenery turns this antique doorstop sheep into a harbinger of Christmas cheer, and warm leather boots add coziness to the corner.

78

Find the hidden lights of
Christmas in unexpected places
throughout your home. When
arrayed with flowers and greenery,
a lovely bottle of perfume glows
as if lit from within.

79

Highlight architectural details in
your home by staying simple
in their trimmings. Here, fir
boughs are entwined with only
soft golden rope for an
understated elegance. ▼

✳ 80

Bring color to every corner:
brighten up a cozy reading
nook with a bold orange or
red amaryllis. ▲

✳ 81

Create a bright and sunny setting
for floral arrangements and treats
by covering a side table with a
small white linen tablecloth. ▼

✳ 82

To enhance a pretty view out a
window, steer clear of tall or dense
arrangements and opt instead to
gather small candles and treasures
on the sill, amid a tender blanket
of holly. ▼ ▼

Outside
the Home

83

Herald the arrival of your
holiday guests by paying as much
attention to an outdoor tree as
you do to your primary tree.
They will feel the warm glow of
your hospitality before they even
turn into the driveway.

84

✳

Gather around a campfire or fire pit to roast marshmallows with family and friends. Enjoy the lovely hush of the snow, and keep warm and cozy with blankets and thermoses filled with hot cocoa.

85

✳

Christen a snow-covered yard
with its own Christmas tree,
reflecting the natural beauty of
the landscape with delicate bird
nests, stars fashioned from twigs,
and a cascade of handblown
glass icicles.

86

✳

Complement the simple
splendor of a winter wonderland
with an ice-blue insulated jug
brimming with paperwhites. ▼

87

Crown a simple porch lantern with a lovely headdress of greenery and a gold-edged organza ribbon.

※
88

Tie bunches of seeded eucalyptus with a pale ribbon to enhance the mystical, historical feeling of these vintage leather skates dangling from a classic old sled painted white, both of which hold many stories of winters past.

※
89

A window box behind the sled boasts a winter "planting" of more cut greenery.

90

Not everyone owns an antique
pony cart, but anything—from
a little red wagon to a yard cart
or a weathered planter—can
overflow with an abundance
of sumptuous greens.

91

Illuminate your front steps by
placing deep red votive candles
into windowed lanterns, casting
fluttering shadows and warm
welcomes onto cold drifts
of snow. ▼

92

✳

On Christmas Eve, light the walk to your home with rows of traditional luminarias, small paper bags filled with enough sand to anchor a votive candle or tea light. Their warm light will gleam in the gloaming and long into the evening, filling the night with Christmas spirit.

93

✳

Mount wreathes in every window to truly transform your home for the holidays.

94

*

When you know Mother Nature will be beautifying your evergreens with a blanket of snow, all you need are bright red velvet bows to create a wonderful Christmas welcome outside your home.

95

✳

Decorate a big red barn with
bright green wreaths, a bushy fir
tree, and plaid satchels bursting
with gifts to bring the promise
of a cozy Christmas.

96
✳

For a bright and exuberant outdoor display, fill shapely painted garden urns with an abundance of seeded eucalyptus surrounded by a profusion of creamy white roses. Carry the touch of silver to your outdoor greens by tucking some eucalyptus bunches there as well.

97
✳

To properly fill garden urns, particularly those of different sizes and shapes but similar floral displays, fit them with watertight liners and plenty of floral foam.

Trim an outdoor trellis with the Christmas hues that nature provides: the red of dried roses and berries, the green of leaves, and the gold of raffia in the winter sunshine.

＊ 98

99

✳

Greet guests with an assembly of gifts sitting on a bench outside, ready to grab. An assortment of classic reads — perhaps early edition hardcovers — are perfect for this.

100

✳

Give your garden a sunny and casual holiday feel, with jaunty little topiary Christmas trees in golden pots, a panoply of bright green plants in terra-cotta, and a lush backdrop of ivy.

101

✳

Take advantage of nature's largess. Line a rock wall or ledge with miniature snowmen and decorate with anything from pebbles to tiny handcrafted scarves and mittens. You can make as many as the snow and space will allow. ▼

Lighting is a vital element to consider when decorating the outside of your home. Be sure your holiday trimmings are all aglow to add warmth and cheer to the long winter evenings.

103

✳

Invite your guests into a woodland-inspired fantasy by lighting the way to your door with candles and pinecones and framing the entryway with lush greenery and an unadorned Christmas tree in a simple concrete planter. ▶

104

✳

Frame pillar candles leading to the door with alternating box-wood and grapevine wreaths and a generous sprinkling of pine-cones. If the night is windy, place the candles in hurricanes or large glass canning jars to keep the flames from blowing out. ▶ ▲

105

Match your exterior decorations to the look of your home. A dense green wreath with a bold red bow is perfectly at home on this bright red door, while something more delicate might appear out of place.

*

Exterior decorations benefit from an eye for detail just as much as indoor trimmings. Tuck a variety of greenery and herbs into a wreath to add color and texture that looks particularly beautiful in daylight against a simple window frame.

107
✳

A light dusting of snow transforms the attractive combination of pine boughs and red velveteen ribbon into a magical harbinger of Christmas spirit. Feel free to spray on your own snow if nature doesn't provide it for you.

108

*

Not all trees can be evergreen. Brighten up the winter landscape around your home with some cheery greenery tied with a bow on a lamppost.

109

When nature's evergreen leaves decorate your yard, a few bright red bunches of holly berries will turn it right into a Christmas wonderland, appreciated by all the members of your family, furry and otherwise. ▼

110

Luscious homemade jams and jellies glow in the afternoon light, creating a perfect picture of warmth and sweetness.

111

Choose outdoor decorations that match the style of your home. This small country cottage is illuminated by a lovely array of tiny lights and candles. ▼

112

Cloak favorite garden statues with holly leaves and berries to bring them into the festivities.

ALL THE TRIMMINGS

Trees

✳

113

Adorn your tree with gifts from the sea. Glue sun-bleached shells, sand dollars, and starfish onto butcher twine for hanging, and be sure to save some to line lanterns on the table.

114

✳

Dress a Fraser fir in wispy blown glass and surround the base with gifts wrapped in airy tissue paper in harmonious hues of violet, pink, and blue for a more ethereal tree.

115

✳

Capture the magical season of sweets and surprises with a tree adorned in the angelic hues of Christmas confections on every bough. Against the deep green tree, old-fashioned ornaments of colored glass in soft pastels seem touched by Jack Frost's wand.

116

✳

Collect vintage hat boxes of various sizes throughout the year for a colorfully original collection of gifts under the tree come Christmastime. Tie them with luminous gold organza.

117

✴

If an item gives you joy, then it will bring joy to your tree. Here, a darling doll skate brings a touch of wistful whimsy to a vintage cellophane tree.

118

✳

Draw inspiration for your decor from classic Christmas stories. This angelic tree dressed in ivory silk roses and silver ornaments was inspired by *The Legend of the Christmas Rose* as told by Selma Lagerlöf, the tale of a flower that blooms white blossoms just for December 25.

119

✳

Lend a breezy motion to your boughs with lustrous streamers of diaphanous organdy ribbon.

120

*

With her porcelain face and organza skirt, this ribbon angel looks beautiful on a tree, but would make a wonderful centerpiece as well.

121

Leave behind the glitter and tinsel and decorate your tree with nature's gifts. Hang an abundance of tiny pots and baskets of fresh and dried flowers, blending in sprigs of rosemary for fragrance.

122

To lend intriguing natural colors and textures to the tree, tuck in boughs of other evergreens, such as silvery acacia and Kelly green cedar. This guest greenery plumps out the boughs and gives the tree as much visual variety as any collection of ornaments.

123

✷

Bedeck your tree with memories from different seasons: a starfish from the beach dressed up with glued-on buttons and set next to a dried-rose heart brings to mind long-lost summer days.

124

✷

Embrace the radiance of white on your tree. Any all-white ornament of graphic shape shows up vividly against green boughs.

125

Get back to the basics for a sweet and simple tabletop tree—done here with popcorn garland, red gingham ribbon, and peppermint sticks tied with twine.

126
✳

Give your tree a folksy bene-
diction with stars handwoven
from wheat. Traditionally, wheat
weavings were believed to bless a
home with good fortune.

127

For a tree abundant with nature's gifts, turn to rich moss balls, plain or painted pinecones, dried fruits, sheer earth-toned ribbons, and a variety of greenery nestled in the branches. ▼

128

Add beloved family heirlooms, like this silver christening cup, as lovely and personal additions to any tree.

129

Brighten your tree and bring
a dream of a white Christmas
right into your living room
with pinecones dusted with
white paint.

130

The rich greens of a Douglas fir are a lovely foil for the hues of handmade sugar ornaments that sweeten the season — like this cupid-painted "hand mirror"— amid pale pink roses and golden pinecones swagged with flowers.

131

For a soothing and elegant theme, try an unexpected palette of soft pastels this Christmas. Instead of sugar ornaments and roses, a tree could be adorned with silk flowers, paper fans, tissue-wrapped favors, and cookies piped with pink and white royal icing for a similarly enticing effect.

132

✳

The little robin on this tree looks right at home, watching over her nest in a natural haven of seeds, berries, pinecones, and a garland woven from sticks.

133

✳

Give your tree a stunning, cohesive theme by limiting your palette to a few choice colors. These ornaments done in white and luminous shades of blue are a lovely reflection of the snow under the bright sky. ▼

134

*

Stock up on Christmas cards that move you or just tickle your fancy. A thin piece of ribbon and two pearl pins can turn any Christmas card into a lovely and personal addition to your tree.

135

*

Add a unique touch of softness, scent, and serenity to your tree with small silk stockings in tranquil pastel colors, stuffed with lavender and decorated with vintage trim.

136

✳

Natural touches like the dried moss ball on this tree can be elegant and sophisticated when hung among twinkling lights with a shimmering champagne bow.

137

*

To maintain a look of elegance and sophistication under your tree, wrap your gifts in an array of colors and textures that complement each other as well as the furniture and decorative details of your room. ▼

138

*

The colors here are so perfectly matched that the beautiful fruits dancing around this tabletop tree seem to have burst forth directly from the painted images on the wall.

139

✳

Nestle a tender nest of faux robin's eggs in your tree to imbue it with the hopeful spirit of nature and rebirth.

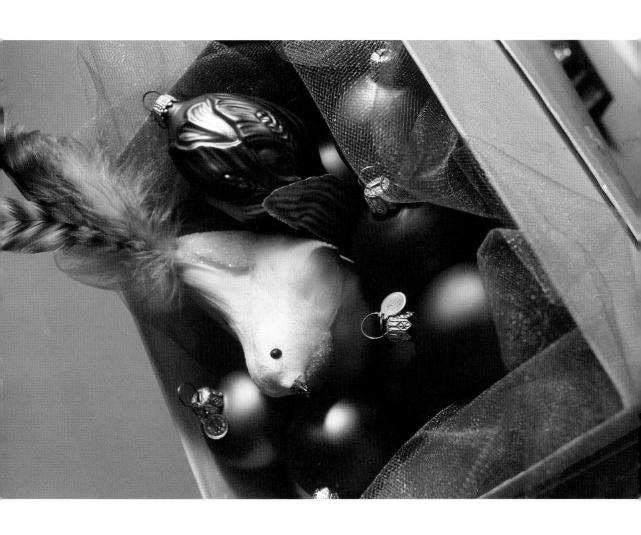

140
✳

Given that they dwell in trees in real life, birds seem particularly appropriate as Christmas tree ornaments. This peaceful dove with a soft feather tail will beautify any tree on which it perches.

141

Bring charm and humanity to your tree with handmade folk art decorations, like this shiny red star made from snipped and painted tin. ▲

142

Transform a tall and stately Fraser fir into a shimmering snow- and star-dusted mountaintop by dressing it with silvery balls, tiny white lights, and dangling clusters of rock candy. ▼

143

*

Envelop your boughs in the cozy warmth of wool with handmade sheep-fleece ornaments.

144
✳

Sometimes less isn't more. This delightful tree is brimming with ornaments, lights, Santas, stories, and an abundance of contagious Christmas cheer.

Wreaths

145
✳

A lush wreath made from a thick swirl of multicolored evergreens needs no fancy adornment. Three clusters of pinecones connected by a thin circle of straw pull it together simply and beautifully.

146

✳

Mount simple birds cut from shiny tin to a wreath wound with twigs and white berries. They become shimmering angels.

147

✳

Tie field bunches of white tallow berries with ribbon and twine to add a snowy winter touch to wreaths, decorations, and table settings. ▼

148

Make a resplendent wreath exclusively from dried herbs, flowers, and berries — there's not a pine needle in sight! Start with a wreath base made of wire, straw, or grape vines and a hook or wire strong enough to hold it. Tightly tuck single-colored batches of herbs and flowers into the wreath base, artfully placing the different splashes of color, and then fill in the gaps with green leaves.

149

Generously deck an open front porch with wreaths, and it becomes even more inviting.

150

✳

Grace your front door with rustic country charm using a wreath of twigs, apples, and lots of bright red berries. ▼

151

✴

Greet guests and carolers with a half wreath adorned in rich reds and russets, densely packed with pinecones on a bed of pine, and balanced with a long leather strip of jingle bells.

152
✳

Wind some graceful twigs into a flowing circle with a few sprigs of tallow berries to imbue a plain farmhouse door with all the joy of the season. ▼

153
✳

Augment a standard wreath with features that add depth and texture. Rhododendron leaves, a few roses, and a touch of holly, topped with an effervescent champagne ribbon, give this entryway an eye-catching twist.

154
✳

Turn a simple dormer window into a warm and welcoming picture of Christmas by adding a thick green wreath adorned with a big red bow. ▼

155
✳

Create a cheerful and appetizing wreath of straw and lots of pale green and yellow apples, topped by a shiny tartan bow. But be careful where you hang it!

Delicate white organza brings with it the appearance of snow-kissed softness and grace to your room when woven into a lush green wreath and flowed through luxurious festoons of garland.

157

✳

Fashion a wreath that is bursting with color and texture. Here, one sees galax and eucalyptus leaves, fir clippings, crab apples, berries, and pomegranates.

158

✳

A wreath woven from an abundance of deep green California bay leaves needs no other adornment.

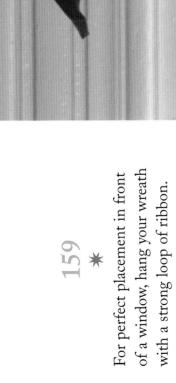

*

For perfect placement in front of a window, hang your wreath with a strong loop of ribbon.

160

✳

Try a wreath in an entirely different shape, such as one that echoes or complements architectural elements of your home. Tightly woven designs of dried flowers and waxy greens create a spectacular effect that will last beautifully throughout the winter.

161

✳

Holly leaves may be prickly to
the touch, but when woven into
a lush, verdant wreath peppered
with their bright red berries,
they become warm and inviting.

162

✳

Experiment with different hues when choosing the evergreen boughs for your wreath. For example, while the sharp needles of a blue spruce deem it an unlikely choice for a Christmas tree, the bright, silvery blue colors of its branches make a wonderful base for a wreath—particularly as a backdrop for bold-colored accents.

163

✳

French doors are a wonderful place to hang an exuberant wreath like this one, full of glowing three-dimensional stars and presided over by an old-fashioned Santa Claus. ▼

164

✳

Give your front door warm country charm by choosing a softer palette for your wreath: dried blooms in pinks and creams and a lacy, straw-colored bow, nestled with pale pinecones in sage-colored branches.

165

✳

Think beyond the traditional circular wreath and discover new and creative ways to adorn your front entrance. The geometric patterns and bronze hue of this door are a perfect backdrop for a triangular Christmas tree done in gold and silver.

Mantels

166
*

Include the four-legged members of your household in your holiday decorations. Create a nook on the mantelpiece dedicated just to them, using cat toys, dog bones, and cozy fleece stockings as whimsical accents. ▼

167
*

Brighten up an ebony mantel and holiday greenery with clean white and pale blue hues. These original glass ornaments and tree toppers are handblown and hand-painted with images of trees, topiaries, suns, and moons.

For the feel of a small-cottage
Christmas by the sea, trim the
mantel with lush greens and
comely shells. Fill an antique
compote with handmade cards
and a shell-covered ball, and
display the most exceptional
finds in a glass cloche.

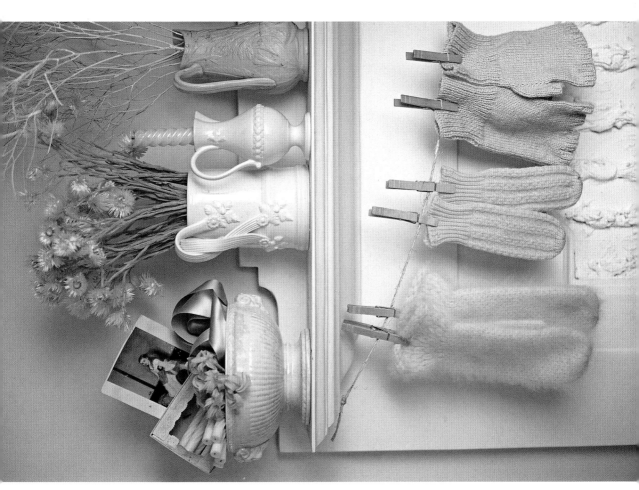

169

*

Create a cozy landscape of whites and creams by hanging handmade woolen mittens from a white mantel holding chunky creamware pieces in the same buttery, warm hues. Embellish with sepia-toned photos, straw-colored dried flowers, and the natural wood of clothespins.

170

✳

Enhance the natural beauty of an exuberant mantelpiece display by lining both the container and the mantel itself with bright green leaves. ▼

171

✳

Bring a look of magical innocence to your mantel with a shimmering star covered in antique German glitter (crushed glass coated with silver) and a sparkling ball of crystal beads and florets. Include a cherished family photo album and a vintage photo on a glass votive candle to add a touch of sentiment.

172
✳

Silver that has been loved for generations gains a mellow patina, and vintage or antique pieces add a sheen and an imaginative touch to any holiday display. On a mantel, a pedigreed creamer, julep cup, and champagne bucket are treated casually as pedestals for pears and a myrtle topiary.

173

✳

Choose holiday trimmings that
work in harmony with the feel
of your home. In this rustic
farmhouse, the mantel becomes
a country-grown surprise, adorned
with scattered seedpods and
greens that seem to tumble out
of a still-life painting and framed
by potted rosemary.

174

Whether they provoke feelings of current excitement or of fond nostalgia, a luminous pair of toe shoes — adorned with silk ribbon and little woven cones of flowers — will add an exquisite grace to any mantel.

175
✳

Install a mantel over an improvised candlelit fireplace to exponentially increase decorating opportunities for Christmas and beyond.

176
✳

Customize stockings with luxurious textures instead of color. These ivory beauties are stitched from vintage Marseilles spreads, damask tablecloths, and eyelet lace.

177

To warm up a regal mantel display, fill in the spaces with subtle textures and colors. Here, an abundance of gold-tipped pinecones and tiny berries scattered among the elegant vases of flowers impart the cozy feeling of a soft forest floor.

178
✳

Center your garnishments around something unexpected, such as a treasured piece like this lustrous antique clock.

179
✳

Give depth to your mantel by layering your decorations, adding a clustering of greenery beneath the ledge that matches the primary garland above.

180

An unadorned magnolia wreath sets a woodsy tone for this mantel, a landscape of muted browns, greens, and gold. The same leaves woven with pinecones and cinnamon sticks make up the sumptuous garland that droops languorously over the edges.

181

Relying on rustic materials and fruits needn't limit one's composition, which always seems helped by using decorative pairs for symmetry: in this case, the miniature pinecone wreaths and two hurricane lamps brimming with spicy potpourri.

182

*

Include a few surprises in your decorations — the kind that bring a personal touch or a smile. Here, amid the birch-wrapped candles and scattering of acorns, we added a favorite pair of old doorstop doggies.

183

For a more formal mantelpiece,
embrace the power of balance
and harmony in the colors and
arrangement of your trimmings.
And pay attention to the details:
here, lovely winter white floral
arrangements are tucked into
elegant Waterford crystal vases,
and candlelight twinkles from
glistening mercury glass votives
and silver candlesticks amid a
sprinkling of tiny gold balls.

184

*

Mirrors make a wonderful backdrop for the flickering lights of candles. This peephole mirror, on loan from the bedroom, also adds architectural interest.

185

*

Try a different take on the traditional shape by creating a square wreath; the deep, rich green of boxwood clippings will lend it a chic elegance.

186

✳

Decorate your home with a series of trees instead of one large showstopper. This stone mantel is a joyous march of diminutive evergreens in cachepots against rich red roses, interlaced with red wooden cranberry garland.

187

✳

Fill clear glass with real whole cranberries to create your own set of holiday-red vases.

188

✳

Turn your hearth into a gardener's joy by filling it with paperwhite narcissus and rosemary, the perfect complement to green-thumbed gifts.

189
✳

Make your mantel magnificent with a luxurious herbal concoction of glycerinated beech leaves, ivy, artemisia, and boxwood.

190
✳

Grace a cherished print or painting with a crown of holiday greenery.

191
✳

Transform your entire mantelpiece into a rich holiday mise-en-scène. This one features Santa bearing many gifts, as well as two woodsmen preparing for the winter. Another figure appears to look on. ▶

Candles

✳

192

Imbue your home with the glow of candlelight and the enchanting aromas of Christmas using high-quality candles scented with oils such as balsam fir, cedarwood, and eucalyptus. Silver votives with red and green interiors can help you illuminate in style.

193

*

Infuse your rooms with a warm natural glow this holiday season. In addition to setting candles on tables and shelves, securely affix hurricane lanterns in windows; turn off all electric lights and enjoy.

194

✳

A small cluster of pillar candles and a millinery cherry branch turn any corner into a cheery nook. Here, candles fill a vintage bird cage with a holiday glow.

195

✳

Transform a simple beeswax candle into a botanical delight by tucking it into a small ceramic pot filled with florist's foam and trimmed with fresh balsam.

196

✳

Surrounding pillar candles with fresh evergreens and herbs is a delight for the senses. They look lovely, and the heat will intensify their fragrance.

197

Beeswax is a wonderful material for decorations because it lasts forever. Scent it with cinnamon, press into patterned cookie molds, and carefully place near a source of heat — the enticing aroma will fill your home. ▼

198

Favors of unrefined beeswax candles send guests home with a fragrant glow. Wrap a pillar or a pair of tapers in pretty paper or fabric — torn edges, as shown, have a romantic appeal. Bind with ribbon, then seal with stamped wax.

199

※

Create a more formal mantel display by embracing the decorative power of symmetry. Here, a perfectly balanced arrangement of candles, ribbons, ornaments, and holly enhance the beauty of the fireplace and give the room a feeling of tasteful elegance. ▼

200

※

Turn a simple candle into a stunning display. Tuck a tall candle holder into a large glass urn and hold it in place with a layer of rich brown chestnuts and a layer of red ornaments that will gleam in the candlelight. ▲

201

※

Bring out the warm tones of woodwork in a living room or study with the glow of multiple candles and bouquets of white flowers. ▼

202

※

Try decorating for the holidays without adding lots of color. Here, large wreaths signal the celebration of the season. ▼

203

Keep the matches in the drawer; with homemade candles this daintily detailed, you will want to enjoy them for years to come.

204

Christmas cookie cutters aren't just for cookies anymore. Fill them with red and green wax and a short wick to create attractive, one-of-a-kind holiday candles. ▼

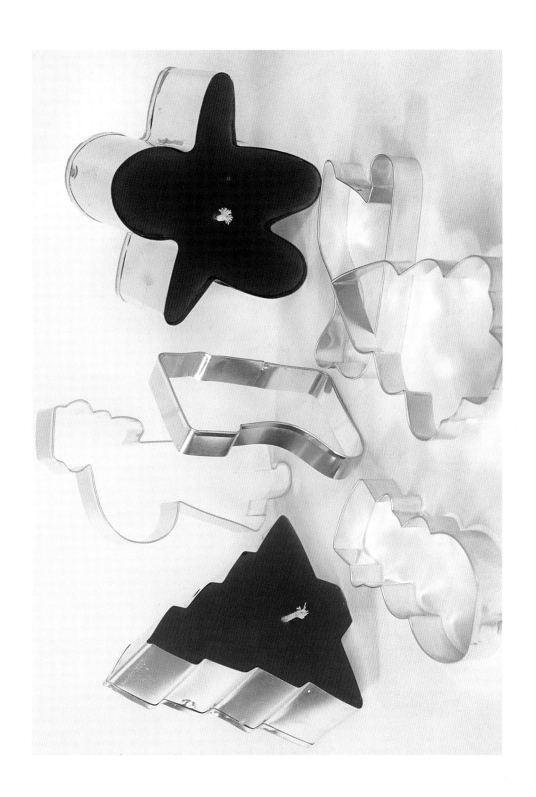

205

Turn plain ivory tapers into glowing beacons of Christmas spirit by encircling them with a rich blanket of leaves and herbs.

206

✳

In the right setting, small ivory votives can take center stage in your decorations. Here, beautiful bronze angels seem to float across a bed of greenery as they present lightly scented candles.

207

✳

Add white bows to any tree to lend a lively touch of brightness. They glisten elegantly in the twinkle of candles and lights.

Flowers

208

✳

To keep flowers looking their best in garlands and wreaths, tuck their freshly cut stems into water-filled florist's tubes and bury the little viles in the greenery. An occasional misting with water will also help.

209

✳

Take garlands beyond mantels and doorways. They look equally handsome emphasizing a window seat, as here, or adorning a chair rail.

210

✳

Sprigs of juniper and lavender sprout from the tender grasp of cream-colored roses nestled in pale ribbon. A bustled lace pillow with silver embroidery is the perfect backdrop for such a delicate Christmas nosegay.

211

✳

These petite blooms seem to
dance with cheer as they burst
delicately from silvery bud vases
that sparkle like icicles. ▲▲

212

✳

Beautifully dress up a simple
straw basket filled with flowers
and holiday greenery with a stately
bow tied with red velvet brocade
ribbon trimmed in gold. ▲

213

✳

For a natural and fragrant
bouquet, mingle pinecones and
dried rose hips in a brown paper
cone tied with thin rope. ▼

214

✳

Hyacinths, spring-blooming
bulbs that can be coaxed to
flower indoors at Christmastime,
can add a wonderful splash of
color and fragrance to your
holiday. In Finland, hyacinths
are considered a classic
Christmas flower.

215

*

Surprise your hosts with an early gift. Hours before the celebration begins, deliver a bouquet of fresh flowers to add a little extra color to their party preparations.

216

✳

Embrace the amazing selection
of flowers available, even in
freezing weather. Try mixing
complementary forms, such
as the pointy petals of lilies
highlighted against shadows
of arching juniper sprigs.

217

✳

Opaque containers, whether
they be wooden boxes, milk-
glass vases, or metal urns, have
the advantage of hiding florist's
foam, which not only holds
water but also anchors stems
for a secure arrangement.

218

Casually arrange clusters of
flowers and herbs; it needn't
be perfectly done. These urns
overflowing with fresh cuttings
from a winter garden look
natural and lovely. ▼

219

✳

Display an exultant profusion
of roses, perfuming the air
and embodying the festivity of
the season, for a Christmas
celebration that announces itself.

220

✳

Give your Christmas greenery
a lift with an unexpected burst
of spring flowers. Here, bright
yellow tulips bring a joyous light
to bunches of seeded eucalyptus
in a 1930s Italian painted vase.

221

✳

When choosing winter flowers,
consider colorful kalanchoes,
whose blossoms come in a
spectrum that ranges from
snow-white and pale yellow all
the way to scarlet and magenta.
Here, *Kalanchoe blossfeldiana*,
known as flaming katys and ideal
for a sunny spot, skirt a pair
of garden finials. ▼

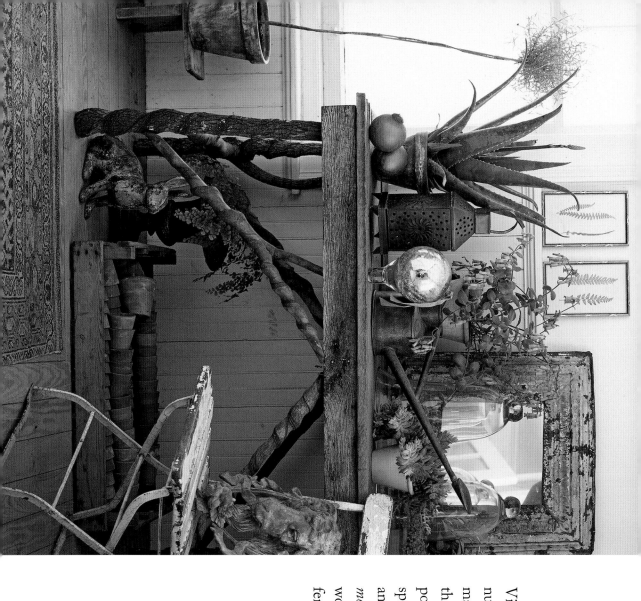

Visit your local florist or nursery to sample some of the many tantalizing alternatives to the classic poinsettia. Here, aloe poised to send up a flower spike, candelabra kalanchoe, and donkey's tail (*Sedum morganianum*) top a handmade wooden table with a maidenhair fern in an urn beneath.

223

✳

Line a staircase with a garden
of potted Rieger begonias, whose
lovely rosebud-like blossoms
will bloom for months, bringing
vibrant color to your Christmas
and the many winter days to
come.

Don't forget to embellish
staircases and hallways. Place
pots of flowers, in the colors of
the season, along the paths you
often take.

＊ 224

225

*

Dress up a tiny side table with a few extravagantly lovely blooms of white amaryllis.

226
✳

Choose flowers with an unexpected hint of elegance to enrich your holiday trimmings. Here, plush velvet roses in chartreuse and plum bring a feeling of plush opulence to a simple glass compote. ▼

227
✳

Draw the lively colors from nature's bounty into glistening glass urns by filling them with handfuls of flower petals.

Creating Atmosphere

228

✳

Enrich the cozy atmosphere of
a quiet study or library with a
simple, unadorned evergreen.
Save the ornaments, the lights,
and the piles of gifts for the other
tree in the busier room; in here,
the rich green boughs and scent
of freshly cut pine perfectly
complement the strong woods,
leather chair, and warm fire for
a mood of peaceful holiday
gratitude.

229

✳

Use decorative touches to bring a small wooden crèche to life. Here, blue ribbons stream down a small artificial tree, embracing the scene like the night sky; a golden filigree star glows when illuminated by candlelight. The mirror behind the scene adds depth.

230

✳

Create a tableau of vintage cards
and treasured family photos to
evoke a strong sense of holiday
tradition. ▲

231
✳

Match creative decorations to favorite winter activities. This tiny *Chamaecyparis thyoides* (a type of cedar), awhirl with bullion wire and glass drops, stands over a mirror ice rink and antique lead skater. ▼

232
✳

Create a Christmas fantasy with decorations that tell their own story. Here, a silver compote holds little mittens, new and old, paired with a miniature knife and fork. The vintage cellophane tree is graced with tiny baby shoes, completing the sweet vignette.

233

✳

Create an aura of old-fashioned romance, letting your best silver pieces bask in warm candlelight, surrounded by lush roses and delicate lace.

234

✳

Enhance the old-world charm of a collection of antique clocks or books by dressing them up with heavy silver candelabras, and a wreath bursting with an abundance of flowers. ▼

235

✳

Place gifts beyond the tree to extend Christmas into every corner—especially gifts wrapped in vintage paper befitting the room's decor.

236

❋

Display delicate pieces of crystal and china under a wreath adorned with pale roses to reflect their gentle hues.

237

❋

Add a lively touch of nostalgia to any display using bright, old-fashioned ribbon candy and tiny winter figurines.

238

❋

In rooms filled with antique treasures like this Victorian silver and Queen Anne sofa, decorate with jubilant swags of flowers, and rich golden ornaments and beads. ▼

239

✳

Warm your shelves with country style: use clothespins to hang traditional paper cones, lined with cozy gingham ribbon and ready to be filled with sweets.

240

✳

Cluster ornate and vintage silver containers and fill them with greenery and a tangle of silvery ribbons and cords too pretty to leave in the trimmings basket. This arrangement gleams beneath a crystal drop girandole.

241

✳

Forego the familiar potpourri of petals and leaves and instead assemble whole bunches of fresh herbs, lavender, dried orange slices, and soft clumps of moss on a big serving platter. The lush blend of colors and textures is as delicious as the aromas that will fill your home. ▼

242

✳

Fill a large glass bowl with a colorful array of handblown glass ornaments — all the same size and shape — for a glistening interpretation of a traditional candy dish.

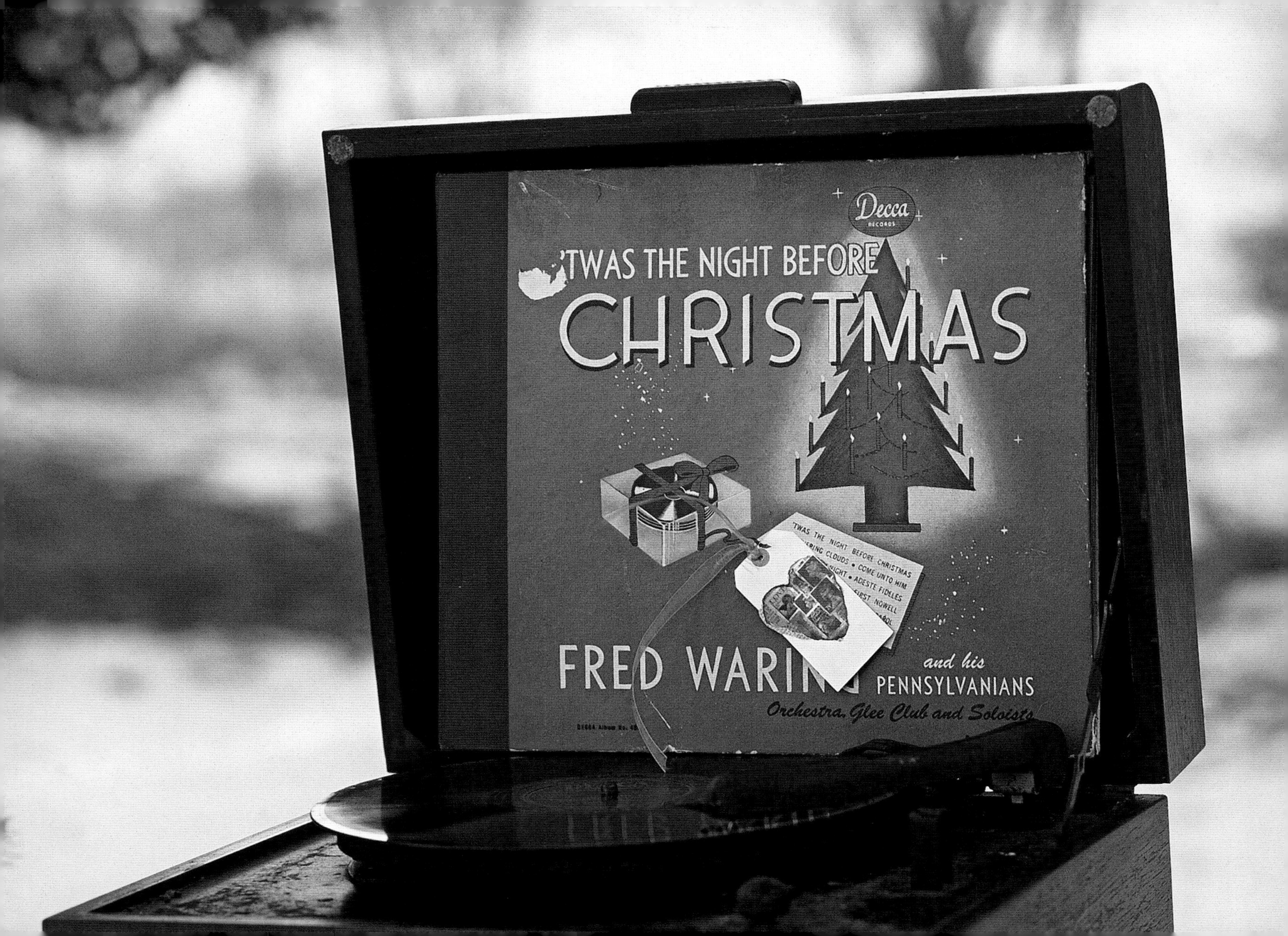
Decca
'TWAS THE NIGHT BEFORE
CHRISTMAS
FRED WARING
and his
PENNSYLVANIANS
Orchestra, Glee Club and Soloists

243

✳

Embrace the ghosts of Christmas Past. Play favorite classic Christmas albums on a vintage turntable. ▼

244

✳

Prop the albums on a wooden ladder with other bygone winter souvenirs like old-fashioned snow shoes and ski poles.

245

✳

A cluster of flickering votive candles transforms this chrome-painted birdhouse into a gleaming cathedral.

246
✻

Serve a Christmas tea fit for
a Georgian aristocrat. Here,
nothing but the finest china
and silver will do in front of a
roaring fire under a mantel lush
with greenery and illumined by
a multitude of candles.

Ethereal heart-shaped wands carry Christmas blessings *en français*, celebrating the year, the holiday, and happiness.

248
✳

Give your holiday decorations
an air of enchantment with
hand-painted, old-world
chalkware figurines.

249
✳

Stage an enchanting winter tableau by gathering a group of figurines on the mantel and including a few dried sprigs to represent snow-covered trees. A mirror behind the scene adds depth. ▼

250
✳

Nothing sets the tone of the season like a warm, crackling fire on Christmas morning. Keep kindling and plenty of long matches handy in twin wrought iron holders.

251

*

Give your Christmas Eve toast an enticing air of romance with mouthwatering chocolates available for nibbling and a juicy slice of strawberry floating in each glass.

252

✳

Transform blown-glass ornaments into fairy tale sweets by gathering them together in a group of clear vessels. Here, we've used urn-shaped apothecary jars, but vases, brandy snifters, and compotes work just as well.

253

✳

Clear glass containers are a wonderful way to achieve a joyous sense of abundance without scatter and clutter. Try filling them with shells, white-painted pinecones, colorful candies, or frosted cookies.

254 ✳

Infuse your home with the ethereal and effulgent color of white. A tabletop tree bedecked with gleaming white cookies and ornaments fills the imagination with magical images of snow and stars and angels.

255 ✳

Embrace the cozy, rustic appeal of a farmhouse-style living room and a wide-planked wooden floor with simple green wreaths and topiaries, a lush and fragrant balsam, and a crackling fire. ▼

256 ✳

A gardener needs no gilt when nature's glow illuminates the tree. For a Christmas tree done with herbs, flowers, and gifts from the garden, choose simple, understated lights to enhance the scene. ▼

257 ✳

Instead of laying a fabric skirt under the tree, strew evergreen boughs to make a soft, green nest for presents — evoking a woodland feel. ▼

258

✳

Gild your holiday with the warm radiance of gold. The opulent glow of these ornaments, multipoint stars, and decorative accents fills the room with a brilliantly festive ambiance.

259

✳

For a woodsy atmosphere with a touch of lasting color, cluster a few decorative pinecones in various textures around a distressed pot of wintergreen (*Gaultheria procumbens*), which holds its bright red berries throughout the winter. ▼

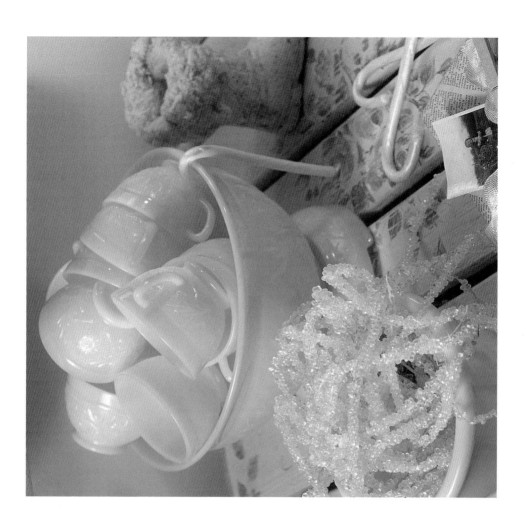

260

✳

If your style is spare, there's no need to make your home feel out of character at Christmastime. Choose a few red and gold accent pieces — even a present or two — to strategically place in an otherwise creamy living room. ▼

261

✳

Gather together favorite items and collections in similar hues for a tableau that is a lovely reflection of you. Here, lustrous hues of ivories and grays fill a side table full of glimmering cheer.

262

✳

Bring the wonderment of a Christmas pageant into your home by setting a scene of three thoughtful wise men ready with their gifts on Christmas morning.

263

✳

Bring serenity and unity to your holiday trimmings with stockings and gifts done in hues that blend with the colors of your home. ▼

FESTIVE GATHERINGS

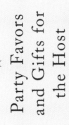

Welcoming Guests

264
✳

Invest in some smart-looking barware to prepare for the lively spirits and parties that are bound to come up throughout the holidays, whether or not you plan them. This stainless steel cocktail shaker and set of double old-fashioned glasses are a perfect party accessory with their jingle bells and bright red leather accents. A handsome tray completes the look.

265

✳

Pamper your holiday guests
with antique linen, one-of-a-
kind guest towels, handsome
bedding, and luxurious linens.

266

Surround guests with touches of elegance, such as antique linen-and-lace tea napkins in shimmering crystal rings and votive candles encircled in hand-tied wire latticework.

267

Spread the joy of Christmas cookies throughout your home: sneak one or two into unexpected places for guests to stumble upon, such as propped against linens and tea towels or tucked behind the creamer for their coffee. ▼

268

Welcome your guests with fresh flowers. Under the watchful gaze of a cloth angel, white roses in a beaded tumbler become a small holiday blessing in the guest room.

269

Turn a guest room into an arresting haven of Christmas enchantment. Deep greens, bold brass, and smart tartan bows are softened by the diaphanous splendor of antique lace curtains aglow in the twinkling lights.

270

Place a small tray of treasures in your guest room to welcome visitors and make them feel pampered. A card, a gift, a single bloom, and a glowing candle will add a special touch to their stay that they won't soon forget.

271

✳

Greet guests—or Santa—with a sideboard arrayed in silver and laden with goodies for later.

272

✳

Turn a Christmas tea into an ethereal experience with an array of deliciously pristine white delicacies, including lovingly decorated snowflake cookies and cupcakes with creamy white icing.

273

✳

Turn a small guest room into a sanctuary of Christmas bliss where visitors can slumber snuggled in red tartan linens, lulled to sleep by the rich scent of pine.

274

To make guests feel pampered,
a little goes a long way. A simple
afternoon cup of hot chocolate
becomes a sumptuous treat when
served with a pair of homemade
cookies and a generous dollop
of whipped cream.

275

A few bright red accents can
turn any guest room into a
Christmas retreat. This sunny
yellow room suddenly glows
with holiday spirit with the
addition of a red throw and
pillows on the bed, a ruby vase
and flowers on the dresser,
and a vivid stack of crimson-
wrapped gifts. ▼

276

Stack linens neatly and wrap them up with a bow, lay them out on a romantic ruffled chair seat cover; they are transformed into decorative objects that make guests feel wonderful.

277

Indulge your overnight guests with herbaceous soaps wrapped in colorful paper and twine. The enticing aroma will pamper their senses whether they use them during their stay or save them for a special occasion. ▼

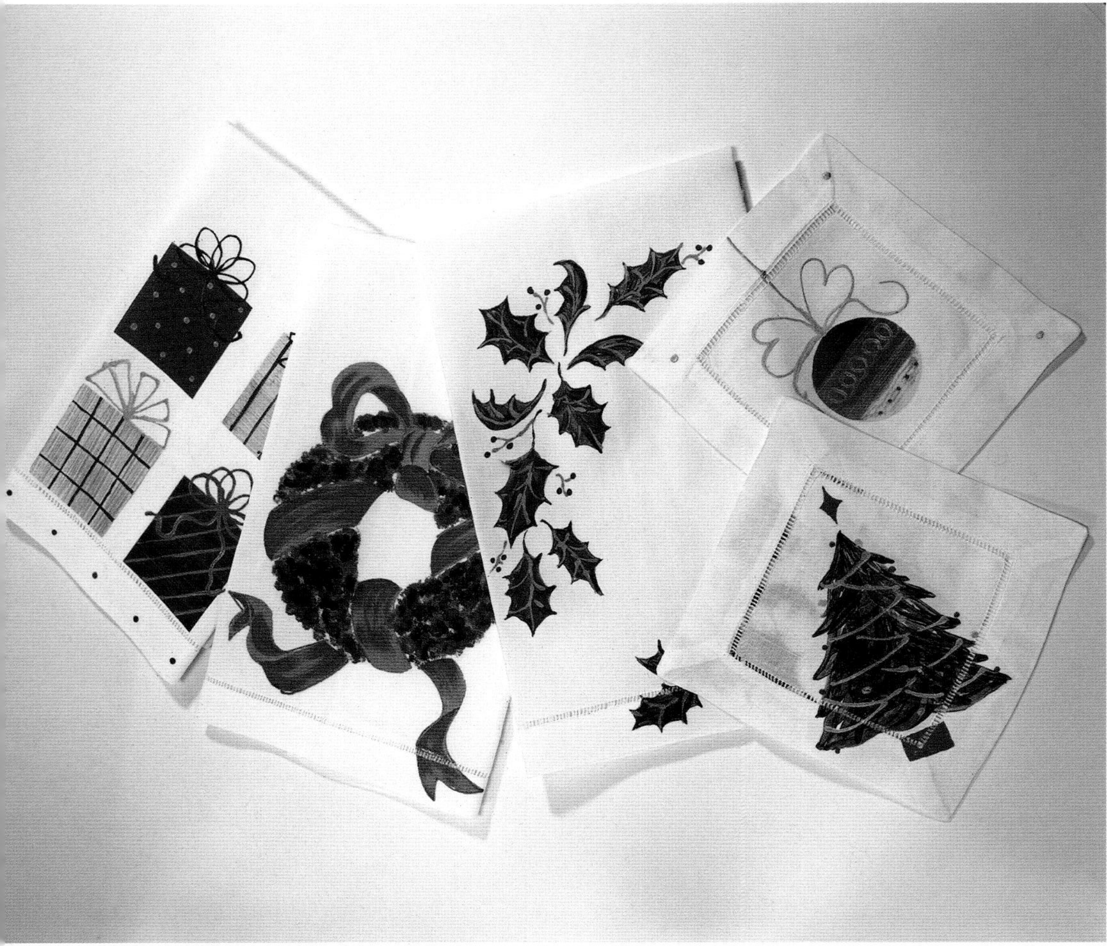

278

✳

Guests may be loath to actually use them, but they will revel in the sincere beauty of hand-painted linen napkins and hand towels.

Gifts Beneath the Tree

279

✳

For a nautical theme, envelop your gifts in fishnet over wrapping paper and finish with string or twine tied in a bowline knot.

280
✳

Transform a gift's wrapping into a charming Christmas keepsake, tying a precious trinket, like this decorative key, into the bows. ▼

281
✳

A fancy wallpaper–covered bandbox is a gift in itself. With glue and sturdy decorative paper, any cardboard box can be turned into an attractive storage piece. ▼

282
✳

Wrap your gifts in nostalgic charm using vintage newsprint tied with lustrous silver rick-rack, glittering snowflakes, and cherished family photos.

Adorn gifts wrapped in handmade paper with a loose pattern of ivy, fragrant arborvitae, and whatever berries you have on hand; anchor with a drop of glue and finish with an ivy vine or a shimmering earth-toned ribbon or rose.

✳

283

284

*

Pepper the gifts beneath your tree with simple family heirlooms, like a classic silver thermos, a worn leather case, and carved wooden paddles atop a weathered trunk.

285
✳

Eschew the traditional ribbons and bows with more creative touches for your gifts, such as homemade paper cut into flower petals and buckles. ▼

286
✳

Some gifts don't need to be wrapped. A lovely hardcover edition of a beloved classic sits perfectly, unadorned, betwixt the branches.

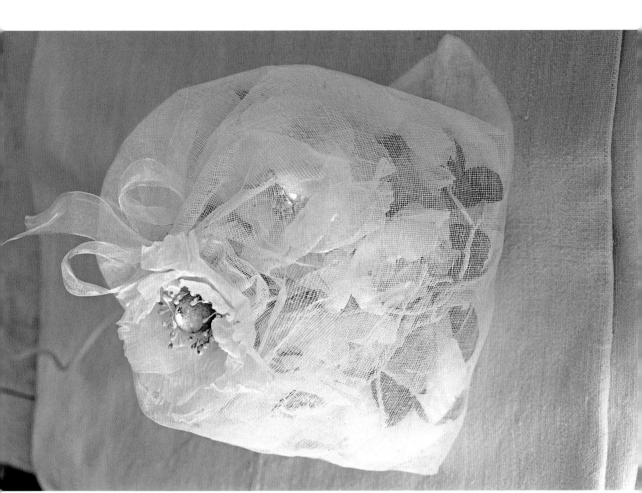

287
✳

A jubilant trio of golden angels
dance across this gift that is
wrapped in a piece of the past:
beautiful calligraphy from a time
gone by. ▼

288
✳

White hand-sewn lace topped
with a glowing canary jewel
and the sheerest of ribbon
provide a delicate shelter for the
mysterious gift tucked inside.

289

✳

Perhaps Santa is making a music request with this lovely violin tucked among the treasures beneath the tree. Its graceful elegance is well-matched by the roses, vintage cards, and shimmering gifts that surround it. ▼

290

✳

Delight any gardener with gifts wrapped in handmade paper and leaves, tied with ivy vines and cypress, and snuggled atop simple earth-toned woolen stockings and brocade botanical pillows.

 291

Try a softer, more gentle palette for your wrappings this year, like this lovely grouping of creams, faded reds, lilacs, and golds.

✳

Sample less conventional color combinations in your gift wrapping. What a nice surprise to discover how perfectly these lavender and periwinkle ribbons complement the classic red and white vintage candy boxes they'll be encircling.

Thinking outside the box can make wrapping — and opening — presents even more joyous. Here, flowers as bows float on hand-painted papers in a palette that trades red and green for fun-and-festive pink and chartreuse.

294

Give your gift easy flair by running ribbons lengthwise instead of the classic crisscross and tucking small gifts, like this powder box, into colorful porcelain tumblers. ▼

295

Heighten anticipation with an imaginative presentation. These gifts, done in unexpected colors, feel like mystical treasures when laid upon a cushion and tied with a soft, iridescent bow.

296

When you fall in love with a particular wrapping paper, get creative. Here, vintage 1950s paper wraps an apothecary jar and covers a tube to form a version of a Christmas cracker. ▼

Add an extra touch of sparkle to a stack of gifts by topping them off with a delicate drape of tinsel and a sprinkle of stars.▶

298

Presents wrapped in gleaming
gold carry sentiments as precious
as the gifts themselves. Glowing
gilt leaves, twisted into a delicate
wreath, add exquisite shimmer
to gifts or on their own.

299

✳

To embellish but not over-power a diminutive gift with an ample bow, choose diaphanous ribbon in a shade that allows the pattern of the wrapping paper to show through.

Little Elves

✳

Shimmering enticingly, a crystalline beaded tree, laden with candy necklaces, swirly lollipops, strips of dot candy (edged with pinking shears), and pretty blue ribbons, tells a magical Christmas story that will delight any little one.

301

✳

What young equestrian wouldn't
love a blue spruce trimmed with
apples, carrots, and lumps of
sugar? This garland is made by
gluing pairs of sugar cubes
around fishing line with a paste
of confectioners' sugar and water.

Create a special children's Christmas corner, where everything is allowed to be touched and placed at just the right height. Here, a clipped boxwood is adorned with toy ornaments and sits near a child-size chair and toys. The tree could also be trimmed with a child's small toys.

303

✳

Give little hands something to do by encircling a dwarf Alberta spruce with wooden train tracks. The snowy base is fleece ribbon, and the tree is decorated with candy-striped chenille garland and silver bells.

304
✳

Pay a graceful tribute to the little ballerina in your home with a feather tree dressed in silk roses with clouds of tulle and chiffon ribbon.

305
✳

Adorn a present fit for a Candyland princess with a fancy, all-sugar fan tipped with sugar paste pansies that seem just picked. You can save sugar flowers and delicacies from year to year by carefully nestling each in cotton and wrapping well to protect them from the damp. ▼

306

✳

Include the handmade ornaments of a child. Nothing exemplifies the spirit of Christmas quite like them, and you'll find they improve all your decorating motifs. ▼

307

✳

Creating a rousing chorus of homemade paper plate orn-aments in red, white, and blue is a wonderful group activity for children, and results in a lively tree full of patriotic as well as Christmas spirit.

308

Tuck several adorable crocheted animals into a small crib or on a chair nestled with pillows — they'll be a sweet set of friends for your younger visitors.

309

Someone dressed Teddy in his best Christmas sweater, so he deserves a place of honor among the trimmings.

Tabletops

✳

310

For a festive look with a touch of whimsy, dress your table for Christmas brunch with silver and gold floral salt and pepper shakers placed alongside a silver watering can votive. A light scattering of white and green flowers will enhance the look without overpowering your simple table.

311

✻

Create a heavenly Christmas Eve table with battery-lit felt angels parading down a glowing table laid with wide, overlapping bands of snowy organdy, Baccarat stemware, miniature crystal hurricane lamps, and individual water carafes evoking old-fashioned milk bottles.

312

✻

Add rich color accents to bring depth to a clean palette of ivories and whites. These luxurious white linens topped with ivory angels, clear glass, and crystal become an elegant and inviting table with the addition of warm orange hues and fresh sprigs of green.

313

✳

Tree ornaments needn't dangle from branches. Use flocked silver-and-white balls, accented by flowers and bright sprigs of green, to add a frosty sparkle to your tabletop. ▼

314

✳

Welcome the Yuletide in regal country style. Gather a cornucopia of fresh fruits to strew among holly boughs as a centerpiece on a holiday table that gleams with antique English candlesticks, china, and glasses. Presiding merrily over this table is a hand-finished replica of an early Italian imp figurine, whose headpiece can hold both candles and flowers.

315

A topiary in a simple terra-
cotta pot makes a stunning
centerpiece for a buffet table.
Dark green myrtle provides a
handsome background for
delicate sprigs of rue and
southernwood and for the
flowers of anise hyssop, garlic
chives, calamint, and big red
roses. The crooked stem adds
charm, and an airy bow
dresses up the pot.

316
✳

Champagne bubbles seem to
float skyward through the delicate
swirls of a pale pink taper.
A snowy tablecloth of white
chenille is the perfect backdrop
for gleaming silver, crystal, and
white decorative accents.

317

✴

Set a winter white holiday table with mismatched place settings of lacy creamware that have both purity of color and variety of pattern. To add more texture, include ornamental doilies tied with delicate silver bows.

318

✴

Decorate each place and enhance a snowy winter theme with shapely white porcelain pears adorned with hand-snipped tinfoil oak leaves.

319

✳

Dress up dessert with garnishes in holiday colors and motifs, such as these whimsical holly leaves in red and yellow.

320

✳

When your table resounds with the splendor of your finest linens, silver, and crystal, be judicious with the extra holiday touches. Here, a few well-placed cream-colored roses and green leaves are all that is needed for a festive holiday look. ▼

321

✳

Give a silk table covering the festive elegance of a ball gown by layering it over Battenburg lace and pulling it into graceful flounces tied with greens, berries, and shimmering ribbon.

322

Grant your eggnog center stage by serving it in a gleaming silver punch bowl and matching silver cups. Surround it with a wreath of cypress and display it with beautiful white linens.

323

✳

Choose a strong accent color to bring together a subtle variety of decorative touches. Here, the bold red of the roses, tapers, and the proud cardinal draw the eye and give a busy table a cohesive theme.

324

Allow Christmas to flow from living room to dining room by carrying the color scheme of your tree onto your table. Here, the flowers and berries chosen for the table's centerpiece echo the sage greens, jewel tones, and lush natural hues of the tree, and the shimmering candles and crystal reflect the tree's twinkling lights.

325

Silver and gold enjoy a regal bond, so Christmas is the perfect time to use them both on the table. Gold-rimmed china and stemware mix beautifully with silver chargers and flatware.

326

*

Embrace an elegant tablecloth with not a hint of red or green. This gold and bronze plaid silk is a perfect choice for the subtle tones and gleaming accents of the table settings.

327
✳

Bring a festive rainbow of color to a table set in neutral tones using a bevy of candied fruit. ▼

328
✳

Top off a joyous place setting of glistening gold-rimmed crystal with one perfect candied pear and a few tiny berries.

A bright red bow enhances the presence of the regal cardinals on this painted china and brings Christmas cheer to each place setting.

330
✳

For a luxurious Christmas feast, an ordinary cheese tray won't do. Place gourmet cheese in crystal stemware atop a nest of rosemary and serve with a full-bodied red wine in an opulent crystal decanter.

331

✳

Embrace originality and create a table that is a reflection of you. Here, a collection of small shells, a lovely nest of speckled faux eggs, and a bright white porcelain apple add lively personality to the classic silver tureen and creamware compote. ▼

332

✳

Allow yourself to fall in love with a beautiful set of vintage Christmas china. Eagerly anticipate that precious moment each year when it is time to take it gently from its box and arrange it lovingly around the table, set days ahead of time so all can admire the heartwarming images of Christmas.

333

This is the season to use gold-rimmed plates that may seem too formal for many other occasions. Be bold when mixing patterns, from the most heavily filigreed to the simplest style. A clutch of dessert forks tied with a swirl of gold ribbon becomes a gift to untie before the conclusion of the meal.

334

Play up gold or silver accents in your china by echoing their hues in a crystal bowl full of ornaments. Mercury glass globes and gold-tipped pinecones add sparkle to any table.

335

✳

Bright touches are warmly welcomed in the depths of a cold winter. Set the table with pewter chargers and goblets, jewel-toned plates and glasses, shed-antler candlesticks, and a frosted robin's egg blue vase filled with tulips to enliven any Christmas reveler.

✳

Use winter white accents on a
table done in the rich reds and
deep greens of your Christmas
best to add light and energy.
Here, the napkins, candles,
and gauzy silk woven into the
greenery carry through the
snowy white of the tablecloth.

337

❋

Dedicate as much care and attention to the trimmings of a buffet table as you would to those for a more formal affair. Here, the luscious colors of the candied fruit, the delicate white china, and the beautifully decorated tabletop tree in a gleaming silver urn turn a Christmas buffet into a splendid occasion.

338

✳

Brighten up your table setting with a hint of sunshine. Tulips and an array of summer fruits will add a twist of sweetness to any Christmas brunch.

339

*

The red and green hues of your favorite botanical china plates are a perfect backdrop for holiday treats. Repurpose your summer china to dish up your Christmas cookies and slices of fruitcake.

This elegant table, replete with divine desserts, features a snowy meringue pie and a colorful assortment of sugared gumdrops nestled in a bed of deep green leaves.

340
✳

341
✳

Candlelight dances across the lovely mélange of sparkling handblown glasses, set for a Christmas Eve champagne toast. ▼

342
✳

Turn simple white linens into a fanfare of Christmas cheer with the brilliant colors of these etched crystal glasses. ▼

343
✳

Find elegance in simplicity: display tiny white desserts on miniature glass cake plates and garnish with a single paperwhite.

344

*

Shelter gourmet cheeses in bell
jars to add an extra dimension
of sparkle to the table.

345

Bring the festive delicacy of white to your gathering by filling polished silver containers with paperwhites and brightening a green wreath with a flurry of spray snow.

346

Enclose pillar candles in glass to add a layer of protection in crowded rooms while making them look more festive.

347

When nestling bottles of champagne and *prosecco* into punch bowls, add a few bottles of sparkling pear cider to delight younger guests.

To make a pleasing centerpiece that's a wintry alternative to flowers, try a textured and aromatic display of hazelnut pomanders tucked in a straw basket among greenery and berries.

349
✳

A three-tiered serving tray filled
with polished Pink Lady apples
does double duty as a lovely red
and green holiday display and as
a crisp and sweet hors d'oeuvre.

350

Transform your tea tray into a delightful vignette. Here, a jaunty ice-skater and two bottlebrush trees on bright red stands are softened by a scattering of hand-molded sugar paste narcissus and roses.

351

When every individual cookie is dressed and decorated with such loving precision, each deserves its own special china plate. ▼

352

Even if it comes right from the carton, serve creamy eggnog in beautiful crystal and china this year, garnishing it elegantly with cinnamon sticks and a dusting of nutmeg.

353

Serving trays are a perfect place to tuck sprigs of greenery and berries and provide any decorated table with a nice focal point. ▶

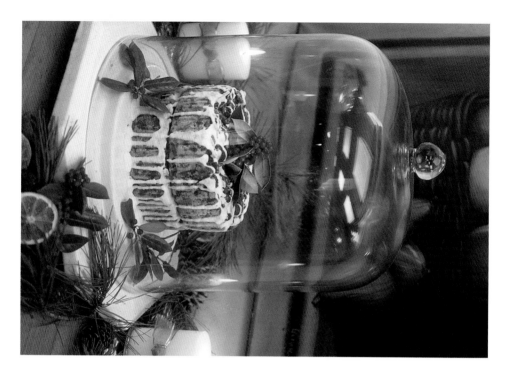

354
✳

Employ glass domes to both protect the food they're covering and to add a lovely twinkle to a candlelit table. ◢▼

355
✳

Infuse your Christmas Eve feast with old-world warmth: wreathe serving dishes with holiday greens and surround them with an abundance of flowers and fruit. ▼

356
✳

Tuck delectable delights like juicy figs into the flowers and greenery of small table arrangements.

Party Favors and Gifts for the Host

357

❋

Present guests (or your hosts) with decadent delicacies befitting the holiday season—French walnut oil, fine peppercorns, and caviar, complete with a silver plate and mother-of-pearl caviar spoon and knife.

358

❋

Welcome your dinner guests with sweetness: on each chair, place a wrapped package of fudge next to a white calla lily.

359

Allow yourself to become enchanted by the romance of the season. Tuck candied almonds or other little delights into gift sachets in delicate floral patterns, tied with sheer white organza and surrounding a shapely toile vase brimming with pastel-hued roses, chrysanthemums, freesia, and greenery.

360

Craft your own gift sacks using a favorite chintz slipcover or a gaily printed forties kitchen tablecloth, worn beyond repair but with salvageable portions still intact.

361

✳

Grace family and friends with personalized Christmas wishes or favorite holiday verses written or typed on high-quality or handmade paper and tied with a simple ribbon. They will cherish them as much as they would any expensive keepsake.

362

*

A gathering of shimmering poppies fashioned from the softest white organdy and gleaming jewel centers waits to grace gifts carefully caressed in linens and lace. ▼

363

*

Tiny glittering silver stars beckon any witness to peer more closely at these chic, gusseted cotton-and-linen bags, sewn by hand and filled with the promises of Christmas.

364

✳

Delight oenophile hosts by delivering your gift of wine in an attractive, reusable package. This tole two-bottle wine tote in pine green and gold brings a touch of history and folk art to the gift.

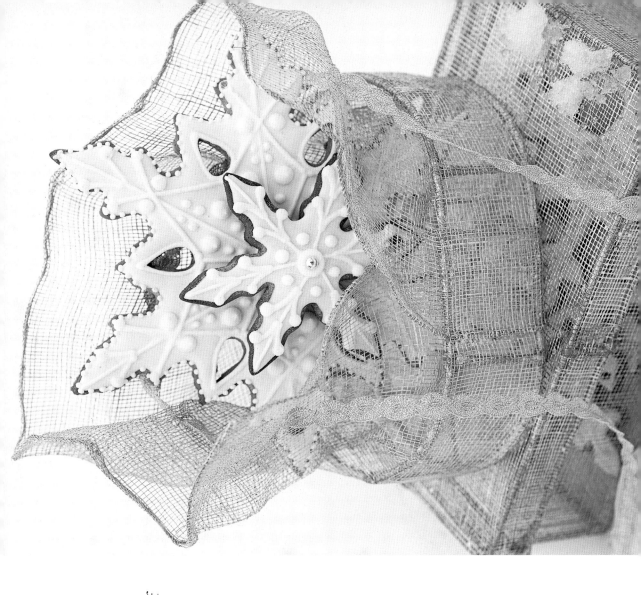

365

✳

Tuck gingerbread snowflake cookies with delicate traceries of white-on-white royal icing into silver mesh drawstring pouches or nesting boxes for an enticing host gift or party favor.

366

*

When attending holiday parties, bring presents with personality and ones that represent the interests and passions of the recipients. A set of glasses featuring swishing skiers is a perfect gift for a family who loves to hit the slopes.

367

*

When you find a host gift you love, stock up. Nothing makes the Christmas party circuit easier than a shelf full of gifts — like these wonderful red pillar candles — wrapped and ready to go. ▼

368

✴

Indulge your hosts with this cheese lover's delight: a hunk or wheel of specialty cheese wrapped in cellophane and served on a wooden cheese board with matching cheese-serving set.

✳

Surround scrumptious party
favors with whimsical accents,
like this beguiling collection of
cerulean blue vases holding
fresh pink roses.

370

Give the epicureans in your
life gourmet delicacies for which
they will be forever grateful,
like decadent white truffle oil
or vinegar made from D'Anjou
pears or late-harvest Riesling.

371
✳

These icy-hued mesh nesting boxes look as fragile as frost on a flocked glass ornament, but they are actually wrought from sturdy abaca fiber. They are a wonderful way to display your gift of cookies or other treats and last long after their wares have been consumed.

372

*

A gift and its wrapping can
be one and the same. For
serenely enchanting party favors,
gather squares of tulle around
handfuls of dried lavender placed
atop cypress and tie into bundles.
Slip fragrant nosegays of cedar
and lavender into the ribbon
bows; they will stand out like
beckoning boutonnieres against
the gauzy white pouches.

373

✳

Delight family and friends with stocking stuffers or party favors that have a distinctive flair. For example, the rustic charm of twig furniture is writ small in these stick pencils, a perfect accompaniment to a stack of handmade cards.

374
✳

Collect vintage lunch boxes throughout the year for a thoughtful and creative way to deliver gifts of holiday cookies. ▼

375
✳

Make your party favors an easy-to-grab part of your holiday decor by adorning them in an array of colorful bows and tucking them into an open wicker basket by the door.

TRADITIONS AND CRAFTS

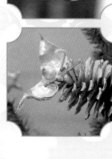

Decorations

376

✳

Fill a vintage tin snowflake cone with handmade incense draped with a plush satin-edged ribbon.

377

✳

Genuine sand dollars and dried starfish are decorating treasures for an ocean-inspired Christmas. Ink them to print images on plain butcher paper for your own custom wrapping paper or make a striking statement by painting them gold or silver. ▶

SKRUDLAND   FEB 62   CHICAGO 34

378

✳

Personalize your decorations with cherished family photos and cards clothespinned with millinery berry branches to a wide blue ribbon.

379

✳

Create a tender altar to Christmas throughout the ages using a treasured family photo, notes and ribbons from a bygone era, a slender terra-cotta heart, and a few touches of nature in wheat and pine. It will warm your home with the history of the season. ▼

380
✳

Turn a festive centerpiece
of pierced creamware and white
roses into a joyful Christmas
card: hang a message in silver
letters on a simple bouquet of
twigs and branches. These letters
were traced on heavy-gauge foil
and attached with silver wire
to keep them from twirling. ▼

381
✳

Delight in little treasures with
long histories, like this dime-
store Santa that has held treats
for Christmas since the 1930s.

382

Decorate a side tree with treats for the taking. Here, packets of shortbread hearts, one for each day of Advent, are illuminated by a constellation of tiny white lights and topped with a multidimensional star.

383

Extend the celebration to outside the home, taking advantage of a snowy setting. A small side table is the perfect spot for a glowing candle and a stash of gifts for the children.

384

✳

Turn an everyday ivy topiary into a gorgeous Christmas showpiece by using small wires to fill it with miniature faux fruits and berries and a smattering of pinecones.

385

✳

Bring vintage holiday flair to a desk or table with the simple addition of a few cherished family photos and letters as well as a spool of elegant gold ribbon.

386

✳

Give your clear glass hurricanes and votive holders the holiday treatment. Cut out paper trees and stars, then tape the shapes to the hurricanes. Spray the entire glass with glue and roll it in artificial snow or glitter so it looks frosted. When the paper is removed, the trees and stars will be transparent, allowing a colored candle within to glimmer through. Come January, a hot, soapy bath will remove the frost.

387

✳

Fill a chunky, painted ceramic mug with a tussle of gingham ribbon, twigs, and berries for some homey holiday charm.

388
✳

These lovely pewter-colored linens pay homage to the Catholic tradition in Provence to serve thirteen desserts at Christmas dinner, symbolizing Christ and his twelve apostles. ▼

389
✳

Reinvent Christmas traditions with gifts from the sea. For Christmas Eve dinner, you can create instant napkin rings by gluing a scallop shell onto thin rope and tucking in a sprig of bay leaves.

390

✳

Gently remove the painting
or mirror that usually sits above
your mantel and fill the space
with a bountiful arrangement of
greenery, pinecones, dried orange
slices, miniature faux apples and
deep red carnations. Eyes will be
drawn immediately to the display,
and no one will notice the
picture hook on the wall, subtly
waiting for the painting or
mirror to be returned after
the holidays.

391

✳

Frame vintage Christmas
storybook covers and illustrations
in lustrous gold or silver for a
one-of-a-kind artistic display.

392

✳

Spell out your Christmas wishes in topiary. Here, the message is simply "angel," written in French.

393

Set a magical Christmas scene by crafting a tiny tree to accompany hand-painted wooden figurines. Wrap a small cup in a beautiful handkerchief and fill it with a batch of ever-green clippings and a few berries, tied with a shining ribbon.

394

Instead of the traditional crèche, embrace a different yet classic mise-en-scène such as this lovely folk art Noah's Ark set with all of the animals, two by two, care–fully carved and painted by hand.

395

✳

Flea markets are wonderful places to find individual Christmas pieces. This unique Santa Claus, in his rugged leather coat and fur Eskimo hat, is ready to brave the frozen tundra.

396

✳

Attach a cluster of twinkling vintage Christmas pins onto a strong silk ribbon for a charming tableau. ▼

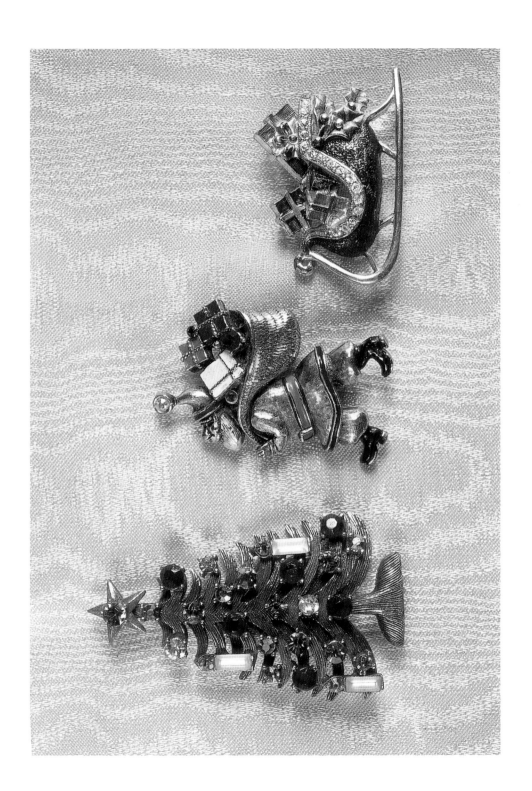

397

*

Stage a charming holiday vignette with jolly Santas working away to ready their bounty of gifts in time for Christmas morning. ▲

398

*

Use soft scraps of vintage fabrics to give homemade stockings the cozy charm of times gone by.

399

Create a lively and natural holiday kissing ball by hot-gluing hazelnuts and rose hips to an orb tucked into a copper pot full of florists foam.

400

Turn the simplest household items into luxurious decorations: the glowing ribbon on this miniature wreath is nothing more than gilded brown paper.

401

✳

Grace your home with natural wonders of your own careful creation. On a cool midsummer morning, collect a batch of unblemished leaves from lamb's ears and gently layer them onto papier-mâché heart shapes using a quick-drying tacky glue. Kept out of direct sunlight, the green leaves will fade to a golden tan and remain intact for years. ▼

402

✳

A handful of offerings from the yard metamorphoses into a dainty white pinecone angel with an acorn face and milkweed pod wings tipped in gold.

403

Old family photos become gems to treasure when they are artfully framed and displayed with handmade garland, greenery, and nostalgic gifts from past holidays.

404

✳

Embrace the delicious charm
of personalized decorations that
reflect your passions. Here, a
homemade ballerina, propped
up by a pair of toe shoes, dances
around a Christmas tree.

405

Intriguing creative details are what give handmade Santas such magical charm. This delightful one is decked out in fur and eager to hit the slopes just as soon as his job is done.

406

Weave cheerful branches of greenery around your puppy's collar; he will wear them proudly, at least for a while. ▼

Ornaments

✳ 407

Embellish your tree with the warmth and nostalgia of visions from a time gone by: scan favorite images from vintage hankies and Christmas postcards, print them onto sheer fabric, and create handmade nosegays, picture frames, and sachets.

✳ 408

Celebrate the wistful beauty of favorite vintage ornaments by wresting them from the depths of the busy tree branches and hanging them singly on a simple structure, leaving enough space around each ornament so that each one is a focal point. ▼

409

✳

Transform plain Manila tags into pleasing individual tree ornaments graced with anything that holds personal memories or meaning, from dried flower petals to colored foil in the shape of a heart.

410

Thread a satin ribbon in an
icy-sherbet shade through
the glass loop of a handblown
ornament for instant shimmer
and a soft, pretty alternative
to ornament hooks.

411

Discover Christmas treasures made by dedicated artisans and craftspeople across the country, like this glistening snowflake painstakingly crafted with tin and time. ▲

✳

Adorn your walls with
homespun simplicity for a
country-style celebration.
Hang handcrafted ornaments
with clothespins on a plain
twine garland, and special
treasures — like these antique
molds used for traditional
springerle cookies — from
colorful plaid ribbon. ▼

✳

Herald the joys of Christmastime in the city with classic silver
bells.

414
✳

Frosted glass ornaments bring a vintage charm and subtle sparkle to your boughs. Hang with a ribbon or thin material cut with pinking shears. ▼

415
✳

A merry Santa dances atop a scattered assortment of greenery, holly leaves, and berries.

416
✳

All it takes to craft an ornament
this exquisite is a carefully
cut pasteboard base, glue, ribbon,
some well-chosen beads, and
a little time.

417

✳

Some of the most treasured toys come to us not from the toy store, but from generations past and from Nature herself. Here, an antique Santa marionette smiles in delight, surrounded by playful royal scepters crafted from dried oranges and cinnamon sticks.

418

Protect your ornaments year to year by storing them carefully in boxes made for that purpose. For smaller trinkets, cardboard egg cartons work nicely as well. ▼

419

Another way to protect your Christmas tree treasures is to keep the box they came in whenever possible. Here, a tray with wells in the precise shape of the ornaments makes for perfect storage.

420

This happy, handcrafted Santa, standing next to a wonderfully busy tabletop tree, clearly agrees that when embracing a fun and imaginative vintage look, there is no such thing as too many ornaments.

421

✳

What could be more cheery
and classic than a vintage hand-
painted Santa and a smile?

422

Trim your tree with treats. Twist and tape squares of heavy white paper into cone shapes, cover with silver paper, finish with a snippet of cord and a tiny ornament, and fill with chocolate stars or other delectable delights.

423

A hand-painted ornament, hung with a delicate wisp of gold ribbon, surprises the tree with sprigs of dill. ▼

424
✳

A trip through the garden,
a can of flat white interior wall
paint, and a dollop of patience
can produce a multitude of
homemade treasures for your
tree. Sweet gum seedpods with
toothpick rays make great stars,
and spiraling wisteria pods
become light-reflecting icicles.
Be sure to use oil-based paint for
pinecones, as water-based paint
would make their bristles close.

425
✳

Trees can light up a room
without the twinkle of lights and
the sparkle of tinsel. The lovely
and striking contrast of white
ornaments in an evergreen tree
creates a luminosity of its own.

426

Honor rural traditions and the old ways of celebrating the holidays. Here, homemade paper ornaments and candy canes deck a tree with nostalgic charm. ▼

427

You don't always need to scour a flea market or estate sale to find old-fashioned ornaments. You can often find them newly minted, like these contemporary versions of Christmas classics, but with vintage charm built right in. ▲

428

✳

Grant a simple, unassuming
ornament a place of honor.
This sweet wooden snowman,
whittled with love and painted
by hand, is highlighted
beautifully by a woodland nest
of pinecones and dried berries.

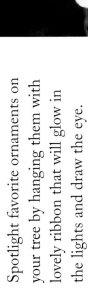

429

✳

Spotlight favorite ornaments on your tree by hanging them with lovely ribbon that will glow in the lights and draw the eye.

may joy & peace & wonder
surround you
throughout the year!

Christmas
Wishes and
Cards

Transform a gift card into
an unforgettable Christmas
keepsake by taking the time to
hand paint each one. To make a
gift stand out even more, try a
cool, glacial palette, tie with old-
fashioned rickrack, and adorn
with a hand-decorated stocking.
They'll never even remember
what was inside the box!

431

✳

Honor gift recipients with tender beaded stars glued to a grosgrain ribbon. Here, the recipient's name is carefully etched onto a small tag.

432

It is said that Christmas is the season of love. Express yours by crafting hearts out of found objects—here, some used stamps applied to an old letter and singed at the edges, dripped pale red wax, and bright red feathers—and turning them into lovely gift tags, ornaments, or place settings. ▼

433

Incorporate Christmas cards into your gift wrap. Whether you find a vintage holiday postcard, like the one shown here, or are offering a card from a current collection, leave the envelope behind.

434
✳

Move away from the everyday place card. Instead, use ribbon to dangle a heart wound of twigs encircling a card with each guest's name or initial. ▼

435
✳

Greet guests with a Christmas card resting on a cozy mitten and propped against a hand-carved birdhouse that's trimmed with holly berries and nestled in the snow.

436

Turn the ribbons on your gifts into harbingers of holiday cheer by embellishing them with personal messages in tiny shimmering beads.

437

✳

For an air of Victorian charm, inscribe your cards and gift tags using a special fountain pen, reserved for the occasion.

438

✳

Keepsake boxes in the same gilded patterns as your favorite ornaments make a handsome statement, as well as a great place to keep treasured Christmas cards.

439

✳

Let your gift clearly display
the love you have put into it by
adorning it with a small red and
gold heart tied with ribbon
and twine. ▼

440

✳

Antique stores and flea markets
are wonderful places to light
upon treasures from Christmas
past. You may have a hard time
letting go of these vintage
Christmas cards, however, as
each precious image is unique
and gathered in a lovely box.

441

✴

Doll up your presents: layer sheer grid paper over pink tissue, weave a lattice of seam binding, and strew with paper flowers.

442

✴

When you've found just the right card, like the leaf and the lily pads shown here, let it be a pretty part of the package as you wrap the gift.

443

*

For a fresh and festive approach to wrapping, raid your sewing basket and your ornament box, grab a glue stick and some double-sided tape, and get creative. Instead of standard ribbon, try a row of metallic daisies or vintage green soutache fluffed with a few inches of pink metallic ribbon.

444

Trimmings of pinecones, holly berries, and a small, vintage model car are a perfect background for this old-fashioned Christmas card with a wistful and heartwarming scene from another time.

Merry Christmas

445

✳

Add a charming personal touch to the table: a name or a simple Christmas wish written on a small white card — one needn't be an artist or calligrapher — gives a beguiling and homey feel to even the most elegantly dressed table.

Natural
Christmas

446
✳

Your home already holds all the elements needed for a comely Christmas display. Fill a simple woven basket with pinecones, greens, and fresh red apples; dust it with snow; and voilà. When it's time to take down your decorations, you can make apple pie.

447

✳

Create a bountiful Christmas centerpiece filled with fresh offerings from your local market. Wire pomegranates, deep red champagne grapes, plums, green apples, and even baby artichokes to floral picks and insert them into a base of damp florist's foam in a terra-cotta pot.

Tuck in red and white roses to enhance the colors and a scattering of herbs to heighten the fragrance.

448

Hang pear and apple shapes covered with seeds on the tree using simple ribbon to evoke the natural feel of a winter garden.

449

To create patterned orange pomanders with the lively look of tree ornaments, dot them with whole cloves in swirled or striped patterns. For a more distinctive look, use a citrus stripper to carve radiating spokes, cascading swirls, or a crosshatched harlequin pattern into the fruit's rind, then insert cloves. ▼

450

✳

Fill your home with the exquisite fragrances of the season. Fashion your own small tree out of box-wood sprigs stuck in a cone of damp florist's foam and decorate it with orange-clove pomanders and a garland of dried cranberries or rose hips. Toothpicks or snips of bamboo skewers work well to hold the oranges in place.

451
✳

Twine miniature wreaths of myrtle around silver candlesticks, accented by a gold ribbon with a hint of red. In the language of flowers, myrtle sends a message of love, peace, and restfulness.

452
✳

Bring the delights of the garden into your home for Christmas. Fill simple wire baskets first with water-soaked florist's foam, then moss (here, sphagnum moss), and, finally, fresh flowers, gatherings, and berries. To last through Christmas, they just need a bit of misting. Try different shapes and sizes for the tree and table decorations. ▼

453

✳

Weave the rich colors, textures, and heady scents of herbs into your decorations. Tuck sprigs of rosemary, signifying remembrance, with an ornament into a tabletop bowl. ▼

454

✳

This convivial basket vibrates with the festive colors of nature. A bow tied with delicate strands of raffia is the perfect finishing touch.

455

Embrace the rustic, homespun feel of the Christmas season. If you have an old barn to decorate and a tree's worth of handcrafted ornaments to set the scene, then perfect. But creating the bucolic spirit of the holiday can be as simple as adding a few touches. Affix jingle bells and a bright red bow onto a much-loved old sled, include handcrafted ornaments made from humble materials on your tree, and nestle gifts into a wooden basket.

456
✳

The heavy wood of a farmhouse table is the ideal backdrop for a rustic setting of heavy earthenware. Organic linens are gathered with a shimmering ribbon and a delicate rose, joining the candlelight to add softness to the scene.

457

Branch out from classic evergreens and fill your home with a multitude of plants and greenery, transforming shelves into fragrant thickets and gracing your rooms with the heady fragrance.

458

For lovely, instant topiaries, start by stripping the stems of a fistful of privet sprigs (or other simple cuttings from a hedge). Braid and wire the stems and stand them in waterproof boxes filled with floral foam and moss.

459

✳

Natural materials will always complement each other, no matter how different their appearance. Amid the sparkle of handblown glass, a star lovingly woven with tender twigs holds its own, lending an air of rustic charm.

460

✳

Holly leaves and berries don't belong only on your wreaths and mantel. Tuck them into the boughs of your tree for an organic splash of color and texture.

461

✳

Turn your centerpiece into a zesty and natural feast of dried winter fruits, filling a woven basket with dried apple slices and whole oranges, gourds of butternut squash, holly berries, and deliciously scented sugar pines.

462
✳

Trim your serving ware with cheerful natural touches. A beguiling bunch of cinnamon sticks tied with raffia and a tiny persimmon sweetens any cookie jar.

463

*

Dress up a natural set of earthenware with some Braeburn apples and bright red berries. ▼

464

*

With a little imagination, any gift from nature's bounty can become a thing of beauty. Here, an armful of birch twigs becomes lovely, frosty filigree for the chandelier.

THE CHRISTMAS PANTRY

414
✳
Cookies

422
✳
Specialties

Cookies

With cookies this colorful and delectable, a cellophane bag and a simple card are all you need to dress them up.

466
✳

Top a Christmas tree sugar
cookie with a real beaded star—
not for eating, please!

467 ✳

When a Christmas cookie is this bright and festive, it deserves a place of honor on the tree. You can enjoy it — picked fresh off the branch — once the gifts are unwrapped. This frosted cookie was artfully adorned with tinted royal icing, sugar crystals, and silver dragées.

468 ✳

White and silver — the colors of snow and bells, Santa's beard, and the twinkle in his eye — adorn this table set with tantalizing holiday treats. Skip the red and green sprinkles this year and decorate all of your cookies and cakes in these shimmering Christmas hues. ▼

469

Pass the cookies and watch them vanish by the tinful. These indulgent takes on a classic have chocolaty batter (intensified with espresso) and chocolate chunks as well. Pack them carefully in cupcake papers and they should arrive intact.

470

Keep an eye out for colorful or vintage tins at shops and flea markets throughout the year. They are wonderful for handing out cookies and treats at Christmastime, turning them into double the gift.

471

✳

These doves-of-peace lemon
cookies (complete with olive
branches) get their depth of
flavor from lemon oil in the
icing. For a celestial gift, wrap
each in sheer tube ribbon, which
you can tie at both ends.

472

❋

As artful as any Florentine angel, these butter cookies, glazed with food coloring, owe their enchanting aura to a delicious dough and exquisite mold — but they'll taste just as good when baked in a simpler shape and left unadorned.

473

❋

Cookies this heavenly must be properly displayed: here, we've propped them onto wispy layers of spun metal and tucked them into a glass bell jar.

474

*

Sometimes the simplest treats are the most satisfying. Here, a basket brimming with tiny and delicious angel cookies beckons, with reliable candy canes and chocolate balls close by.

Specialties

475

A Christmas morning delight, this apricot-and-almond breakfast wreath is fragrant with cinnamon and bursting with dried, candied Australian apricots. Ring it with shiny red berries on a white china compote for a bright breakfast centerpiece.

476

✳

Present herb- and cranberry-flavored vinegars in glass decanters. They can be as gorgeous as they are aromatic; a splash of the cranberry is delicious on fresh fruit. You can start making these well before the rush, since they last for four months.

 477

Nuts have been a holiday tradition since families roasted their own on the hearth. These honeyed sesame soy nuts have a delicious spicy flavor you won't find anywhere else. Serve them in these individual foil baking cups or fill a paper cornucopia ornament to hang on a friend's Christmas tree.

*

Cranberry-orange conserve, if packaged in a painted Moroccan glass, looks festive enough to go right on the table. Almost a chutney, the conserve is spicy with ginger, cloves, and cinnamon and dense with bits of blood orange, nuts, and raisins. It's a delicious foil for the Christmas goose or turkey and just as lovely with cold meats.

✳

479

Dazzle the gathering with a festive Yule log, or *bûche de Noël*, complete with cupcake knots. This version is made just like a layer cake (no rolling). The fun is sculpting the side frosting as bark, the top as tree rings!

480

*

A sparkly tangle of silver wire
and stars illuminates simple
ramekins of crunchy delicacies,
like these rum-flavored fritters
called *oreillettes*, or "little ears."

ULTIMATE CHRISTMAS

481

✳

Studded with tart, dried cherries, the chocolate brioche loaf is light in texture but rich in flavor—and ideal tea loaf. The cherries (you could also use cranberries) lend tang to every bite.

482

✳

Create patterned parchment paper with a special paper punch, as show here, or try an embosser or rubber ink stamp.

483

∗

Blended with fresh-snipped herbs and crusted with pistachios, goat cheese has never tasted so delicious. This special cocktail hour savory is an excellent gift for any host or hostess —you can give it before the parties start. Or bring it along to one, complete with its own glass cheese dome and knife.

484

Use heart and star shapes and chunks of chocolate to make these candies a treat for two senses. After tempering bittersweet and white chocolate, pour it into molds and top with crushed peppermint.

485

To double your dose of glad tidings, tuck distinctive treats into memorable packaging. For instance, some boxes come with labels that may be monogrammed with any initials you'd like.

486
*

Baked with cranberries and crystallized ginger, this lovely shortbread will satisfy sweet tooths of every size, and little ones especially. Scout around at tag sales and flea markets for an old-fashioned shortbread jar to give it in.

487

✳

Cheddar sticks and rounds are
an inspired choice for piquant
tastes — cayenne pepper and
sesame seeds impart extra zest.

488

✳

Silver mint julep cups can
become chic serving pieces and,
swathed in cellophane, a gracious
gift wrap.

489

Fill a candy jar or pretty patterned box with homemade meringue mushrooms; either way, they're guaranteed to disappear more quickly than the real thing. Fun to make — and eat — these whimsical treats are apt to fool all but the most experienced eye.

490

To appease the diet gods—but indulge a friend—consider a pair of healthy, low-sugar favorites: a granola mix (with dried blueberries, apricots, and almonds) and a trail mix (a blend of roasted nuts and cherries, cranberries, blueberries, and raisins). ▲▲

491

Treat your friends and family to the delectable combination of chocolate with a colorful crown of fruit and nuts, tucked in silver corrugated boxes or other pretty little packages. These clusters contain apricots, cranberries, golden raisins, and slivered almonds. ▲

492

✳

Offer up special homemade confections with a flourish: tie them with handmade paper and copper twine and display with antiqued gilded fruit on a three-tiered cake stand.

493

✳

Give your holiday marmalade a unique sweetness by adding the richness of dried Australian apricots.

✳

Make a tantalizing coffee cake from a classic sour cream recipe. Light and moist with a crunchy top, it's perfect for breakfast by the tree.

✳

Nestle sweet slices of candied mandarin in glass bowls encrusted with trompe l'oeil ice crystals. ▼

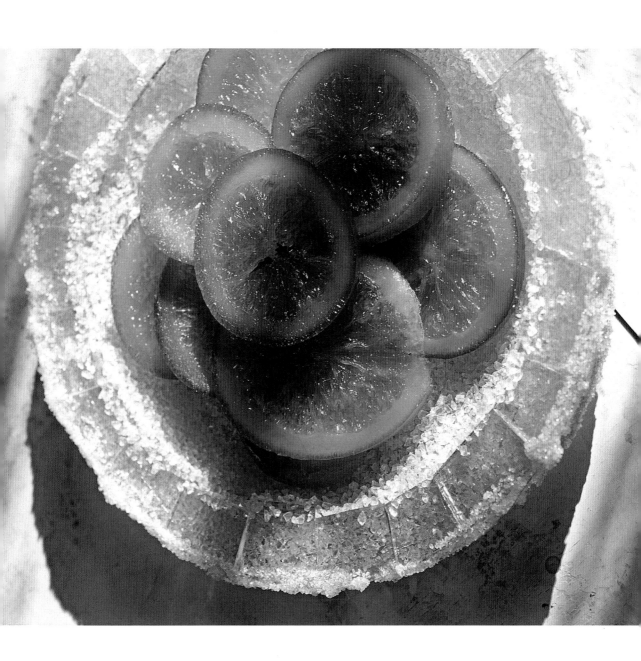

* 496

No trifles, these truffles, but richly appreciated gifts. The creamy, dark chocolate nuggets are spiked with peppermint for holiday flavor and lightly dusted with cocoa. They look especially tempting in a translucent little organza gift bag with a ribbon drawstring; just be sure to line the bag with cellophane first.

497

A platter of *pfeffernüsse* — sugar-dusted spice cookies — glows in candlelight like freshly driven snow under a full moon. ▼

498

Classic butterscotch sauce is even better chunked with roasted macadamia nuts — or any nuts you choose. All that's lacking is the ice cream to drizzle it over. Bring it to a host or hostess in any lidded bowl you've collected, such as this Depression-era glass sugar bowl. ▲

499

Turtles may be poky, but these chocolate caramel turtles will scoot off the plate. A simple secret: start with ready-made caramels and melt them. Include a nice serving plate, such as this lacy creamware one, and you've doubled the gift. Try wrapping the whole in cellophane before tying artfully with ribbon.

500

Transform a homemade dessert into the gift it is meant to be: present it wreathed with greenery and encircled by a shimmering organdy ribbon. ▼

RECIPES

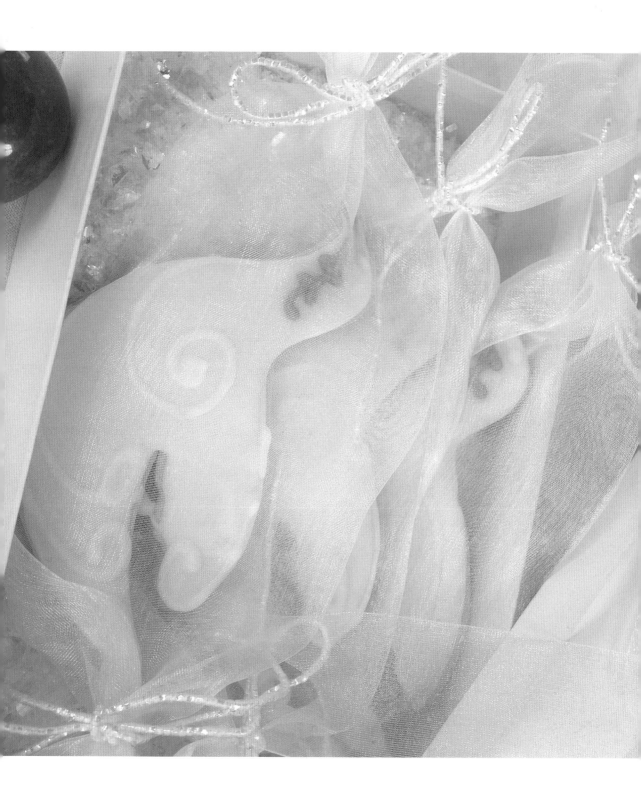

✳ Lemon Cookies ✳

In one bowl, whisk together the flour, baking powder, and salt. In a separate bowl, with an electric mixer on medium, cream the butter and add the sugar a little at a time, until light and fluffy. Beat in the egg a little at a time, the vanilla, and the lemon zest until just combined. Add the dry ingredients. Divide dough in half and wrap each half in plastic, flattening into a disk. Chill 1 hour.

Preheat the oven to 350° F. Line baking sheets with parchment paper.

Working with half of the dough at a time (keeping remaining dough chilled), roll out dough between sheets of lightly floured wax paper to ⅛ inch thick. Stamp out cookies with floured cutter. Transfer to prepared baking sheets. Bake cookies for 8 to 10 minutes, or until pale golden around the edges. Let stand on the sheets for 5 minutes, then transfer to racks to cool completely.

Make the icing: In a bowl, whisk all ingredients together until smooth, adding a little water if too stiff. Decorate the cookies with the icing and let dry.

Store in airtight containers for up to 2 weeks if unfrosted, 1 week if frosted. Makes about 2 dozen cookies, depending on the size of the cutter.

2 cups all-purpose flour
½ teaspoon baking powder
½ teaspoon salt
1 stick (½ cup) unsalted butter
⅔ cup sugar
1 large egg, lightly beaten
1 teaspoon vanilla
4 teaspoons finely grated lemon zest

FOR THE ICING
2 cups confectioners' sugar
1 large egg white
½ to 1 teaspoon lemon oil, available at specialty food stores

✳ Chocolate Caramel Turtles ✳

60 pecan halves
8 ounces caramels
1 tablespoon heavy cream
6 ounces tempered dark or milk
chocolate (see recipe opposite)

Line a baking sheet with parchment paper. Arrange 5 pecan halves for each turtle, 1 for the head and 1 for each limb. Leave a little space in the center of each cluster for the body. Arrange nut clusters about 2 inches apart.

In a small saucepan set over moderate heat, combine the caramels and heavy cream and heat, stirring, until caramel is just melted. Remove pan from the heat. With a spoon, fill in the center of each turtle with the caramel, being careful to leave the outer tips of the nuts uncovered. Temper the chocolate (see the directions on next page) and spoon over the caramel, again being careful to leave the outer tips of the nuts uncovered. Let cool completely until hard. If desired, before the chocolate is set, use the back of a small knife to make crosshatch marks to resemble turtle shells. Wrap individually in cellophane.

Store in a cool place for up to 1 week. Makes 12.

✳ Tempered Chocolate ✳

In the top of a double boiler set over simmering water, melt the chocolate until it reaches a temperature between 88° and 90° F. This is the "tempered" chocolate.

Pour ⅔ of the chocolate onto a cold surface such as marble or a chilled countertop (place ice-cube trays on counter to chill it). With a spatula, spread the chocolate on the cold surface until it reaches a temperature of approximately 81° F. Add the tempered chocolate to the untempered chocolate and mix well, until it reaches a uniform temperature.

✳ Butterscotch Sauce ✳

In a heavy saucepan over moderate heat, combine the sugar, corn syrup, water, and butter, and simmer, stirring occasionally, until a candy thermometer registers 189° F.

Add the vanilla and salt and stir vigorously until combined. Add the cream and cook, stirring occasionally, until smooth. Add the nuts. Let cool and transfer to a jar or container with a lid. Chill. Sauce keeps one month in the refrigerator. Makes about 2 cups.

⅔ cup firmly packed light
　　brown sugar
2 tablespoons light corn syrup
½ cup water
6 tablespoons unsalted butter
2 teaspoons vanilla
½ teaspoon salt
½ cup heavy cream
1 cup coarsely chopped toasted
　　macadamia nuts

✳ Chocolate Brioche Loaf ✳

2½ cups all-purpose flour

⅔ cups unsweetened
Dutch-process cocoa powder

1½ teaspoons baking soda

¾ teaspoon salt

2 large eggs, lightly beaten

1½ cups sugar

6 tablespoons unsalted
butter, melted

1 cup sour cream

1 tablespoon espresso powder

1 tablespoon vanilla

1 cup dried cherries or cranberries

1 cup toasted, coarsely
chopped walnuts

Preheat the oven to 350° F. Butter a 9- by 5- by 3-inch loaf pan.

In one bowl, whisk together the flour, cocoa powder, baking soda, and salt. In another bowl (large), whisk together the eggs, sugar, butter, sour cream, espresso, and vanilla. Add the dry ingredients to the liquid, a little at a time, stirring, until combined well. Fold in the dried cherries and nuts. Transfer batter to the pan, smoothing the top.

Bake for 1 hour, or until a cake tester inserted in the center comes out almost clean (the center should still be a little wet). Let stand in pan for 10 minutes, then transfer to rack to cool completely. Wrap in plastic and chill.

May be prepared 5 days ahead.

Serve at room temperature, garnished with sifted confectioners' sugar. Makes 1 loaf.

✳ Cranberry and Blood Orange Conserve ✳

In a large saucepan over moderately high heat, combine the sugar, vinegar, spices, and water. Bring to a boil, stirring, and simmer until sugar is dissolved. Add the citrus zests and fruit and simmer 10 minutes more. Add 2 cups of the cranberries and the cranraisins and simmer, stirring occasionally, for 30 minutes. Stir in the remaining cranberries and simmer, stirring occasionally, for 15 minutes. Stir in the nuts.

Let cool, transfer the conserve to sterilized jars, seal with lids, and process in a water bath for 10 minutes. Cool, tighten lids and store in a cool, dark place for up to 1 month. Makes about 4 cups.

2 cups firmly packed light
   brown sugar
½ cup cider vinegar
1 teaspoon ground cinnamon
½ teaspoon ground ginger
½ teaspoon ground clove
1½ cups water
1 lemon, zest grated, pith removed,
   fruit cut between membranes
   into sections
4 blood oranges, zest grated from
2 oranges, pith removed,
   fruit cut between membranes
   into sections
4 cups cranberries, picked over
   and rinsed
1 cup cranraisins or raisins
1 cup chopped toasted nuts

1 pound cranberries
4 cups rice vinegar
Peel from 1 navel orange,
  excluding pith

✳ Cranberry Vinegar ✳

In a bowl, crush the cranberries. Add the vinegar and orange peel, and let stand, loosely covered, in a cool, dry place for 3 days. Strain mixture into a saucepan and bring to a boil. Pour mixture into a decorative sterilized bottle and let cool. Add a corkscrew of orange peel to the bottle for garnish. Store in a cool, dry place for up to 3 months. Makes 1 quart.

✳ Dark Chocolate Peppermint Truffles ✳

In a saucepan, combine the cream, salt, and vanilla bean, scraping the vanilla bean seeds into the cream and straining. Simmer, then cool. In another bowl, combine chocolate with butter. Stir until smooth. Stir in the cream mixture and peppermint oil. Cover and freeze until firm.

With 2 melon ballers, scoop out 1-inch balls of chocolate. (Use 1 melon baller to scoop out chocolate balls and the other to dislodge the chocolate from the first.) Roll the ball in the cocoa powder until completely coated. Continue forming truffles in the same manner. Transfer truffles to a container and chill, covered. May be prepared one week ahead. Makes about 30.

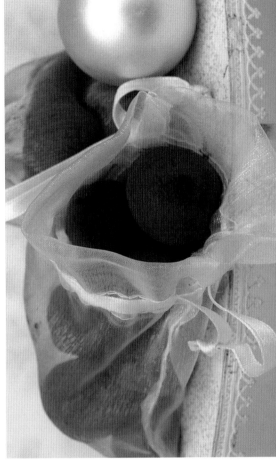

⅔ cup heavy cream

1 vanilla bean, split lengthwise

A pinch of salt

8 ounces dark sweet chocolate, melted

1 tablespoon softened unsalted butter

½ teaspoon peppermint oil, or to taste, available at specialty stores

½ cup unsweetened Dutch-process cocoa powder for coating the truffles

✳ Pistachio-Crusted Goat Cheese ✳

1 pound fresh goat cheese, softened

3 tablespoons softened unsalted butter

2 tablespoons each snipped fresh chives, minced fresh tarragon, and minced fresh parsley leaves

1½ teaspoons each minced fresh thyme or lemon thyme leaves and minced fresh rosemary leaves

Salt and freshly ground pepper to taste

⅔ cup shelled, skinned pistachios, chopped fine

In a bowl, blend the cheese, butter, herbs, salt, and pepper until combined well. Form the mixture into six rounds and coat each in the pistachios. Wrap individually in plastic and chill for up to 1 week. Makes 6 rounds.

✳ Spicy Sesame Soy Nuts ✳

Preheat the oven to 350° F. In a large bowl, combine the soy sauce, 1 tablespoon of the sesame oil, butter, honey, and salt. Add the nuts, sesame seeds, and cayenne pepper and toss to coat. Transfer the nuts to a shallow baking pan and bake in one layer, stirring once, for 15 to 20 minutes, or until golden brown and fragrant. Add remaining sesame oil, toss to combine and let cool. Transfer to jars or containers with lids and store in a cool, dark place. Nuts will keep up to 2 weeks. Makes 3 cups.

3 tablespoons soy sauce

2 tablespoons Asian sesame oil

1 tablespoon unsalted butter

2 teaspoons honey

1 teaspoon sea salt

2 cups roasted, unsalted nuts

1½ tablespoons toasted
    sesame seeds

⅛ to ¼ teaspoon cayenne pepper,
    or to taste

✳ Double Chocolate Espresso Cookies ✳

½ cup all-purpose flour

½ teaspoon baking powder

½ teaspoon salt

1 stick (½ cup) softened unsalted butter

⅓ cup granulated sugar

⅓ cup firmly packed light brown sugar

2 large eggs, lightly beaten

1 tablespoon espresso powder

1 tablespoon vanilla

8 ounces bittersweet chocolate, melted

1 cup bittersweet chocolate morsels

½ to 1 cup chopped nuts, such as walnuts or pecans

Preheat the oven to 350° F. Line baking sheets with parchment paper. In one bowl, whisk together the flour, baking powder, and salt. In another bowl, with an electric mixer on medium, cream the butter, add the sugars a little at a time, and beat until light and fluffy. Add eggs, espresso, and vanilla. Reduce speed to low and add the chocolate and flour mixture a little at a time until blended. Stir in nuts.

Drop the batter by rounded tablespoons onto the prepared sheets, spacing them 2 inches apart. Bake for 10 to 12 minutes, or until dry on the outside but still soft in the center. Let stand on the sheets for 5 minutes and transfer to racks to cool completely. Store in airtight containers for up to 1 week. Makes about 2 dozen cookies.

✳ Bûche de Noël ✳

FOR THE CAKE

1½ cups cake flour

1 teaspoon baking soda

½ teaspoon salt

⅔ cup unsweetened cocoa, preferably Dutch process, such as Droste

⅔ cup boiling water

1½ sticks (¾ cup) softened unsalted butter

1 cup granulated sugar

1 cup firmly packed light brown sugar

2 large eggs, lightly beaten

2 teaspoons vanilla

½ cup sour cream

Preheat the oven to 350° F. Butter two 7-inch springform pans. Line with wax paper, and butter and flour the paper, shaking out excess flour. Butter well two individual muffin cups.

In a bowl, whisk together cake flour, baking soda, and salt. In a saucepan, combine the cocoa with the boiling water. Whisk until smooth. Let cool.

In another bowl, with an electric mixer, cream the butter. Add the sugars a little at a time. Beat until fluffy. Add the eggs a little at a time and the vanilla. Finally, beat in the cocoa mixture just until combined well. Add the flour mixture alternately with the sour cream to the butter mixture, ending with the flour.

Fill two muffin cups ⅔ full with the batter and divide the rest of the batter between the two cake pans. Place the cake pans and muffin pan in the oven. Remove the muffin pan after 15 to 18 minutes, or when a cake tester inserted in the center comes out clean. Let muffins cool in the pan for 5 minutes. Invert onto racks to cool completely. Wrap in plastic and chill.

Make the frosting: In a saucepan, combine the cream, butter, corn syrup, cocoa and salt. Simmer, whisking. Add the chocolate and let stand 5 minutes. Add vanilla and whisk until smooth. Cool to spreading consistency.

Halve each cake layer horizontally and sandwich with frosting. Frost top and sides of cake. With a round cutter, make "knots" from muffins, cut bottoms of knots on the diagonal, attach to the sides of the cake and frost. With the tines of a fork, create patterns to resemble tree bark and tree rings. Decorate with shaved chocolate and dust with confectioners' sugar if desired. Chill, loosely covered, up to 4 days. Serve at room temperature.

FOR THE FROSTING

1 cup heavy cream

1 stick unsalted butter, cut
   into tablespoons

⅓ cup light corn syrup

⅓ cup unsweetened cocoa,
   preferably Dutch process,
   such as Droste

A pinch of salt

12 ounces melted dark
   sweet chocolate

1½ teaspoons vanilla

✳ Angel Butter Cookies ✳

2 sticks (1 cup) softened unsalted butter

1¼ cups sugar

1 large egg, lightly beaten

1½ teaspoons vanilla extract

4 cups all-purpose flour, plus extra for dusting mold

A pinch of salt

Vegetable oil

For the glaze, if desired:

1 cup confectioners' sugar

3 to 4 tablespoons water, or as needed

Liquid food coloring

EQUIPMENT

Ceramic angel mold

In a bowl with an electric mixer, cream the butter and sugar until fluffy. Beat in the egg and vanilla. In another bowl, sift together the flour and salt. Add dry ingredients to the butter mixture slowly, beating until just combined. Do not overmix. Form dough into a disk, wrap in plastic, and chill 5 hours or overnight.

To prepare mold: Chill angel mold. Lightly brush mold with vegetable oil, coating all crevices and indentations. Wipe away excess oil with paper towels. Sift flour over the mold, tipping it back and forth, until it is evenly coated. Hold mold upside down and lightly tap against a surface to remove excess flour. Flour mold before making each cookie, but do not re-oil.

To mold dough: Break off a piece of chilled dough large enough to fit into the mold. (Leave remaining dough in refrigerator.) Gently knead dough in your hand 2 or 3 times to smooth out wrinkles. Press dough quickly into the mold while it is still cold and slightly stiff. When mold is completely filled, press dough to remove air pockets and form an even cookie. Carefully press any dough extending over the edges back inside the form. The cookie should not be thicker than the mold. Use a large knife to trim dough flush with the edge of the mold.

To unmold cookie: Rap the edge of the form repeatedly against a wooden board, rotating mold at the same time. When the cookie is loosened all over, tap or gently peel it out onto a baking sheet. If the dough sticks to the mold, carefully loosen with the point of a paring knife. Prepare remaining cookies in the same manner, spacing them 2 inches apart on the cookie sheet. Chill while preheating oven.

Preheat oven to 350° F. Bake cookies for 8 to 11 minutes, or until lightly golden around the edges. Let cookies cool on sheet for 5 minutes, or until firm enough to handle. With a wide spatula, transfer cookies to wire racks and let cool completely. Cookies can be eaten plain or glazed.

To glaze cookies: In a small bowl, combine confectioners' sugar with enough water to form a glaze. Divide glaze among small bowls and tint with food colorings. Cookies can be brushed with a single glaze or painted with different colors, using paint brushes in different sizes. Makes about 8 cookies.

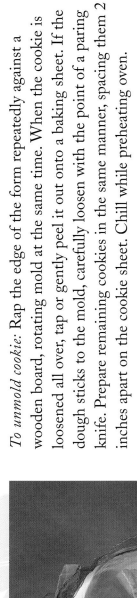

✳ Cranberry Shortbread ✳

2 sticks (1 cup) softened
    unsalted butter
½ cup superfine sugar
2 cups all-purpose flour
¼ cup cornstarch
¼ teaspoon salt
⅔ cup coarsely chopped
    dried cranberries
¼ cup minced crystallized ginger

Line one large or two small baking sheets (to accommodate three 6-inch rounds) with parchment paper.

In a bowl with an electric mixer, cream the butter and sugar until light. With the mixer on low, add the dry ingredients slowly, and the cranberries and ginger, mixing just until crumbly. Transfer dough to a lightly floured surface. Gently knead until it just comes together. Divide dough into three balls and transfer to baking sheets, pressing each into a round about 6 inches in diameter. With a large, sharp knife, cut each round into eight wedges. Do not pull sections apart. With a small knife, score the edges of each round to create a scalloped edge. With the tines of a fork, decoratively score the top of the dough. Chill for at least 15 minutes.

Preheat oven to 350° F.

Bake the shortbread for 25 to 30 minutes, or until edges are lightly browned. Let cool for 15 minutes and transfer to racks to cool completely. Shortbread can be cut into wedges while warm or kept in rounds to be cut at serving time. Makes 24 cookies.

Cranberry Shortbread ▼
Chocolate Peppermint Bites ▼ ▼

✳ Chocolate Peppermint Bites ✳

6 ounces good-quality bittersweet
chocolate, tempered
(directions on page 447)

6 ounces good-quality white
chocolate, tempered

1 cup crushed peppermint candy

Have ready heart-shaped and star-shaped plastic candy molds. Temper the dark chocolate. Pour a very thin layer of the dark chocolate into each mold. Let cool 10 minutes. Temper white chocolate. Pour a very thin layer of white chocolate over the dark chocolate. Sprinkle with peppermint. Chill until set. Makes about 24 candies.

✳ Spicy Cheddar Wafers ✳

6 ounces sharp cheddar, grated

6 tablespoons unsalted butter, cut into bits

⅔ cup all-purpose flour

½ teaspoon salt

⅛ teaspoon cayenne pepper, or to taste

1 egg yolk

An egg wash made by beating 1 egg white with 1 teaspoon water and a pinch of salt

3 tablespoons black sesame seeds, or a combination of black and white sesame seeds

In a food processor, combine the cheese, butter, flour, salt, and cayenne. Process with an on-off action until mixture is combined. Add the egg yolk and process until mixture just comes together in a ball.

Preheat the oven to 375° F. Line baking sheets with parchment paper.

Pinch off 1-inch pieces of the dough, roll between palms to form balls, and flatten balls to ¼ inch thick. Arrange rounds 2 inches apart on baking sheets, brush tops with egg wash, and sprinkle with sesame seeds. Bake for 12 to 15 minutes, or until crisp and golden.

Alternatively, pinch off 2-inch pieces of the dough, roll between palms to form 6- to 7-inch logs, and transfer to baking sheets. Brush tops with egg wash and sprinkle with sesame seeds. Bake for 12 to 15 minutes, or until crisp and golden.

Cool on the sheets for 5 minutes, then transfer to racks to cool completely. Store in airtight container for up to one week. Makes about 12 dozen wafers, or 1 dozen logs.

✳ Orange Marmalade ✳ with Dried Apricots

3 large Valencia or navel oranges
1 large lemon
3 cups water
3 to 4 cups sugar
½ pound dried apricots, diced

Remove the peel from oranges and lemon, being careful not to remove white pith. Cut peel into slivers. Remove pith from oranges and lemon. Halve each, and remove and discard seeds. Cut oranges and lemon into dice, being careful to reserve juice, and transfer to a large heavy casserole or kettle. Add 3 cups water and simmer uncovered for 10 minutes. Cool and let stand, covered, overnight.

Measure fruit mixture. For every cup, add a scant 1 cup sugar. Return to casserole and bring to a boil, stirring, until sugar is dissolved. Boil gently, stirring occasionally, for 25 minutes. Stir in apricots, bring back to a boil, and boil for 10 to 15 minutes more, or until a candy thermometer registers 218° to 220° F. Skim off the froth, stir for 1 minute and ladle into sterilized ½ pint jars, filling to within ⅛ inch of tops. Wipe off the rims and seal jars. Cool, check seals and labels, including date. Store in a cool, dark, dry place. Marmalade keeps for about three months. Makes about 4 half pints.

✳ Meringue Mushrooms ✳

¾ cup sugar

¼ cup water

3 large egg whites, at
room temperature

⅛ teaspoon salt

⅛ teaspoon cream of tartar

½ teaspoon vanilla

Sifted confectioners' sugar for
sprinkling on the mushrooms

For forming mushrooms, either:

About ⅔ cup melted chocolate or
1 recipe Chocolate Ganache
(directions on next page)

Sifted unsweetened cocoa for
sprinkling on the mushrooms

In a heavy saucepan set over moderate heat, combine the sugar and water and bring to a simmer, swirling the pan and washing down the sides of the pan with a brush dipped in cold water, until sugar is dissolved. Boil the syrup, undisturbed, until a candy thermometer reaches 240° F (soft-ball stage).

In the meantime, in a bowl with an electric mixer, beat the whites with the salt until foamy. Add the cream of tartar and beat the whites until they form soft peaks. With the mixer running, add the sugar syrup in a stream, and continue beating the meringue for 8 minutes, or until cool. Beat in the vanilla.

Preheat the oven to 200° F. Line 1 to 2 baking sheets with parchment paper. Transfer meringue to a pastry bag fitted with a ¼ inch plain tip. Pipe 40 small mounds onto the paper, each about 1 inch in diameter. Then, holding the pastry bag straight up, pipe 40 cones on the baking sheets, to be mushroom stems. Dust caps and stems with confectioners' sugar and bake for 2 hours, or until completely dry.

Make mushrooms in one of two ways

For mushrooms that will last up to two weeks in airtight containers: Use melted chocolate as glue. Dip stem tip into melted chocolate and attach to mushroom by pushing chocolate-covered tip into bottom of cap. Let dry.

Or for mushrooms filled with Chocolate Ganache, which will last up to one week if kept chilled in tightly covered containers: After 1½ hours baking time, remove sheet from oven and gently push in the undersides of the mushroom caps. Return to oven and bake for 30 minutes more. Turn off heat, and let stand in oven overnight. Transfer Chocolate Ganache to a pastry bag fitted with a ¼ inch fluted tip, and pipe the cream into the undersides of the caps to simulate gills. Push a stem into each cap, and chill until ganache is firm.

Before serving, lightly dust the mushrooms with sifted cocoa powder. Makes about 3 dozen.

CHOCOLATE GANACHE

In a small saucepan set over moderate heat, bring the cream just to a simmer. Have chocolate ready in bowl. Immediately pour the hot cream over the chocolate and stir until melted and smooth. Chill until firm enough to pipe. Makes about 1¼ cups.

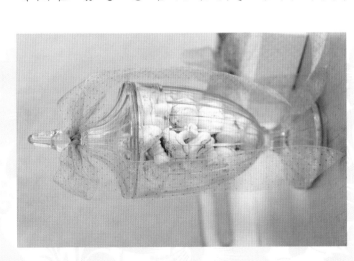

½ cup heavy cream
6 ounces dark sweet chocolate, chopped

✳ Toasted Granola with Dried Fruits and Slices Almonds ✳

4½ cups old-fashioned rolled oats
1 cup wheat germ
1 cup raw sunflower seeds
1 cup sliced almonds
1 cup sesame seeds
1½ tablespoons ground cinnamon
1 cup honey
½ cup orange juice
¼ cup canola oil
1 tablespoon grated lemon peel
1 tablespoon grated orange peel
¼ teaspoon salt
2½ cups dried fruits, such as blueberries, diced apricots, cherries, and cranberries

Preheat oven to 325° F.

In a large shallow baking pan or two medium shallow baking pans, combine the oats, wheat germ, sunflower seeds, almonds, sesame seeds, and cinnamon.

In a small saucepan, combine the honey, orange juice, oil, lemon and orange peels, and salt. Cook, stirring, over low heat until mixture is smooth. Pour the honey mixture over the oat mixture and toss until ingredients are coated. Spread into even layers and bake, stirring frequently, for 35 to 40 minutes, or until golden brown and toasted. Let cool 5 minutes. Stir in the dried fruits. Granola can be stored in airtight containers for up to 2 months. Makes about 10 to 11 cups.

Toasted Granola with Dried Fruits and Slices Almonds ▶
Fruit and Nut Clusters ▶ ▼

✳ Fruit and Nut Clusters ✳

½ pound good-quality bittersweet chocolate, tempered (directions on page 447)

½ cup combination of dried fruits and nuts, such as dried pieces of apricot, cranberries, golden raisins, roasted and salted cashews, almonds, pistachios, and hazelnuts

Line a baking sheet with parchment paper. Using a tablespoon, drop the tempered chocolate onto the paper, holding the spoon about 2 inches above the paper and letting the chocolate drip off the spoon. It will form natural rounds. Top each round with some of the dried fruits and nuts.

Place the baking sheet in the refrigerator and chill clusters for 30 minutes, or until hardened. Store clusters between sheets of parchment or wax paper in a cool, dry place. Fruit and nut clusters keep for 3 days. Makes about 18 clusters.

✳ Sour Cream Coffee Cake ✳

FOR THE FILLING AND STREUSEL TOPPING

¼ cup firmly packed light-brown sugar

¼ cup granulated sugar

1 cup toasted pecans

2 teaspoons cinnamon

½ teaspoon salt

¼ teaspoon freshly grated nutmeg

½ cup finely diced Australian glacéed apricots or similar dried apricots

½ cup cake flour

6 tablespoons unsalted butter, cut in bits

½ teaspoon vanilla

Preheat oven to 350° F. Butter and flour a 9-inch springform pan.

Make filling and topping: In a food processor, combine the sugars, nuts, cinnamon, salt and nutmeg. Process until nuts are coarsely ground. For filling, place ¼ cup of nut mixture in a bowl and stir in the apricots, making sure they do not clump. Set aside. To the remaining topping, add the flour, butter, and vanilla. Process till crumbly. Transfer to a bowl.

Make the batter: Sift the flour, baking powder, baking soda, and salt into a bowl. In another bowl with an electric mixer, cream the butter. Add the sugar a little at a time and beat until light and fluffy. Add the eggs slowly and the vanilla. Alternately beat in the flour mixture and sour cream, starting and ending with flour.

Transfer one third of the batter to the pan and sprinkle with half the apricot filling. Add half the remaining batter and sprinkle with remaining filling. Add the rest of the batter. Distribute topping evenly over batter. Bake for 50 to 60 minutes, or until a cake tester inserted in the center comes out clean. Let cool in the pan, remove sides, and transfer to a serving dish. Before serving, dust with confectioners' sugar. Cake will keep, wrapped in plastic, for up to one week. Makes 1 cake.

FOR THE BATTER

2 cups cake flour

1½ teaspoons baking powder

½ teaspoon baking soda

½ teaspoon salt

1½ sticks softened
   unsalted butter

1 cup sugar

2 large eggs, lightly beaten

1½ teaspoons vanilla

1 cup sour cream

Confectioners' sugar for
   dusting cake

PHOTO CREDITS

Page 139: Jim Bastardo
Page 140: Jim Bastardo
Page 141: Toshi Otsuki
Page 142: Toshi Otsuki
Page 143: Guy Bouchet
Page 144: Toshi Otsuki
Page 145: Jeff McNamara
Page 146: William Steele
Page 147: William Steele
Page 148: William Steele
Page 149: Robert Kent
Page 150: David Montgomery
Page 151: Toshi Otsuki
Page 152: Toshi Otsuki
Page 153: Toshi Otsuki
Page 154: Susie Cushner
Page 155: Susan McWhinney
Page 156: Susie Cushner
Page 157: Toshi Otsuki
Page 158: Jim Bastardo
Page 159: Jim Bastardo
Page 160: Toshi Otsuki
Page 161: Toshi Otsuki
Page 162: Toshi Otsuki
Page 163: Toshi Otsuki
Page 164: Toshi Otsuki
Page 165: Toshi Otsuki
Page 166: Charles Maraia
Page 167: Charles Maraia
Page 168: Charles Maraia
Page 169: Charles Maraia
Page 170: Charles Maraia
Page 171: Charles Maraia
Page 172: William Steele

Page 173: Toshi Otsuki
Page 174: Susie Cushner
Page 175: Toshi Otsuki
Page 176: Toshi Otsuki
Page 177: Toshi Otsuki
Page 178: Toshi Otsuki
Page 179: Toshi Otsuki
Page 180: Guy Bouchet
Page 181: Laura Resen
Page 182: Toshi Otsuki
Page 183: Toshi Otsuki
Page 184: William Steele
Page 185: Toshi Otsuki
Page 186: Toshi Otsuki
Page 187: Toshi Otsuki
Page 188 (left): William Steele
Page 188 (right): Toshi Otsuki
Page 189: Toshi Otsuki
Page 190: Toshi Otsuki
Page 191: Susan McWhinney
Page 192: Toshi Otsuki
Page 193: Toshi Otsuki
Page 194: Toshi Otsuki
Page 195: David Prince
Page 196: David Prince
Page 197: David Prince
Page 198: David Prince
Page 199: Luciana Pampalone
Page 200: Toshi Otsuki
Page 201: Toshi Otsuki
Page 202: Susan McWhinney
Page 203: Tara Sgroi
Page 204 (left): William Steele
Page 204 (right): Tara Sgroi

Page 205: Toshi Otsuki
Page 206: Toshi Otsuki
Page 207: Toshi Otsuki
Page 208: Toshi Otsuki
Page 209: Toshi Otsuki
Page 210: William Steele
Page 211: Toshi Otsuki
Page 212: Toshi Otsuki
Page 213: Toshi Otsuki
Page 214: Toshi Otsuki
Page 215: Toshi Otsuki
Page 216: Toshi Otsuki
Page 217: Michael Skott
Page 218: Guy Hervais
Page 219: Toshi Otsuki
Page 220: Toshi Otsuki
Page 221: Susan McWhinney
Page 222: Susan McWhinney
Page 223: Toshi Otsuki
Page 224: Toshi Otsuki
Page 225: Toshi Otsuki
Page 226: Susan McWhinney
Page 227: David Prince
Page 228: David Montgomery
Page 229: Toshi Otsuki
Page 230: Toshi Otsuki
Page 231: David Montgomery
Page 232: Steve Randazzo
Page 234: Susan McWhinney
Page 235: Susie Cushner
Page 236: Susie Cushner
Page 237: Susie Cushner
Page 238: Guy Hervais
Page 239: Toshi Otsuki

Page 240: Toshi Otsuki
Page 241: Toshi Otsuki
Page 242: Toshi Otsuki
Page 243: Guy Bouchet
Page 244: Toshi Otsuki
Page 245: Toshi Otsuki
Page 245: Susan McWhinney
Page 246: Jim Bastardo
Page 247: Susie Cushner
Page 248: Toshi Otsuki
Page 249: Toshi Otsuki
Page 250: Toshi Otsuki
Page 251: Toshi Otsuki
Page 252: Toshi Otsuki
Page 253: Tara Sgroi
Page 254: Jim Bastardo
Page 255: Guy Hervais
Page 256: Toshi Otsuki
Page 257: Toshi Otsuki
Page 258: Toshi Otsuki
Page 259: Steve Randazzo
Page 260: Christina Schmidhofer
Page 261: Christina Schmidhofer
Page 262: Christina Schmidhofer
Page 263: Christina Schmidhofer
Page 264: Luciana Pampalone
Page 265: Luciana Pampalone
Page 266: Tara Sgroi
Page 267: Tara Sgroi
Page 268: Tara Sgroi

Page 269: Tara Sgroi
Page 270: Tara Sgroi
Page 271: Toshi Otsuki
Page 272: Toshi Otsuki
Page 273: Toshi Otsuki
Page 274: Susie Cushner
Page 275: Toshi Otsuki
Page 276: Susan McWhinney
Page 277: Guy Hervais
Page 278: Toshi Otsuki
Page 279: Toshi Otsuki
Page 280: Toshi Otsuki
Page 281: Toshi Otsuki
Page 282: Toshi Otsuki
Page 283: Michael Skott
Page 284: Toshi Otsuki
Page 285: Toshi Otsuki
Page 286: Toshi Otsuki
Page 287: Toshi Otsuki
Page 288: Toshi Otsuki
Page 289: Toshi Otsuki
Page 290: Toshi Otsuki
Page 291: Toshi Otsuki
Page 292: Toshi Otsuki
Page 293: Toshi Otsuki
Page 294: Toshi Otsuki
Page 295: Toshi Otsuki
Page 296: Toshi Otsuki
Page 297: Susan McWhinney
Page 298: Toshi Otsuki
Page 299: Toshi Otsuki
Page 300: Jim Bastardo
Page 301: Susan McWhinney
Page 302: Jacques Dirand

474 Photo Credits

INDEX